D0931024

HAPPENING
DESIGN FOR EVENTS

Frame Publishers
Amsterdam

Birkhäuser – Publishers for Architecture
Basel / Boston / Berlin

CONTENTS

TV commercials, radio jingles, drab newspaper ads, the predictable full-page spreads in glossies – no one gives them a second thought any more.

INTRODUCTION

You Make It Happen

Go-go dancers toss their tresses in wild abandon. Pulsating flashes of coloured light bounce off every surface, and projected images fill the bare walls of the former factory hall with bright abstract patterns. The DJ's ear-splitting house beat crashes into the steel roof of the Amsterdam venue and reverberates throughout the space. Underlining the feel of an extraordinary evening is a guest list limited to an in-crowd of local journalists, musicians, designers and other creatives. People are talking, dancing, seeing and being seen. A sudden wave of excitement grips the room. A dozen brawny, leather-jacketed bikers thunder into the hall on humongous Harleys, engines roaring. Seated behind each 'angel' is a leggy transvestite balancing a gleaming tray of timely hors d'oeuvre – an appetizing but inedible display of watches, one for each guest. About three years ago, I attended this grandiose party, which took place in an exuberantly decorated factory warehouse in Amsterdam. Music, song, theatre, dance – the event was an all-out effort to embellish the introduction of a new watch, although the product launch was almost overshadowed by the spectacle itself. The evening was a colourful collage of creative disciplines. Over half a century ago, the American artist Allan Kaprow organized similar gatherings, at which theatrical performances, works of art and music, and the liberating hubbub of a party merged to provide a titillating experience. Because the guests themselves played an active role at such get-togethers, invitations went out to a select company of like-minded individuals. It was what you might call 'an extraordinary evening for the local in-crowd'. This was where it was all happening, and to emphasize the fact Kaprow called his parties 'happenings'. Although the product launch in Amsterdam had little in common with Kaprow's gatherings, it was nonetheless a genuine happening.

The world of the happening is one without borders. A happening has to fascinate a global audience.

Sometimes it's easier to get people's attention with a veiled whisper than with a piercing shriek.

Thus a successful happening is not a self-absorbed spectacle but, on the contrary, an invitation. The only requirement is you. Without you, it's not an event.

The music may have changed from jazzy improvisation to the programmed pump of house, and works of art may have been replaced by delectable designs – even the theatrical entrance of rumbling Harleys was more streetwise than academic – but here, too, was an orgy of miscellaneous artistic endeavours rooted in the spirit of Kaprow's happenings. Admittedly, the event in Amsterdam relied on applied arts; even so, it aroused emotions that ran the gamut from astonishment and glee to annoyance and a tinge of fear.

An obvious choice for the title of a book on the high-profile events being staged today is Happening. For that matter, the same word applies to the publication of the book itself, for event design is definitely what's happening at the moment. Brand marketers, in particular, have discovered it as a vehicle for drawing attention to a product. TV commercials, radio jingles, drab newspaper ads, the predictable full-page spreads in glossies – no one gives them a second thought any more. They're ageing forms of 20th-century advertising. Experience marketing is the way to a prosperous future. The presentation of a new watch is no longer done with a large-scale poster campaign. Instead, the manufacturer pampers a trendy slice of who's who with watches dished out by leggy transvestites.

Experience marketing is not about what you have to say but about how you say it. Translate that into the world of design and 'form follows function' suddenly becomes 'form is function'.

This book offers the reader a total of 29 irresistible events. And if anything is made clear in these pages, it's that at least 29 types of happenings exist – from fashion shows and pop concerts to automobile launches and trade-fair openings. To maintain some sort of order, the makers of the book have divided the subject matter into themes: fashion, audio, auto, sport and culture. The difference in categories is not always apparent, however; after all, predictability can spell disaster for what is meant to be a rip-roaring event.

Who is the event designer, anyway? Don't look for the answer to that question in this book, because the event designer is a nonentity. Dutch event outfit Wink, for example, began as an organizer of hip dance parties. Knock, based in Sweden, is more of a contemporary ad agency that uses the event primarily as a marketing tool. Schmidhuber +

Partner of Germany is a multifaceted architecture firm that can fulfil the needs of its client – Samsung, in this case – with both an office design and a futuristic reception centre at the Olympic Winter Games in Turin. All sorts of event designers are making their presence known, each with an individual approach to the task at hand. The world of the happening is one without borders. A happening has to fascinate a global audience. A multicultural example is one in which the Dutch firm Wink designs a show for Italian fashion label Diesel, which will take the show to Bread & Butter, a trade fair in Germany. But wherever they come from and whatever their approach, all event designers have a habit of blithely browsing through the entire catalogue of creative disciplines to transform even the most minor non-event into an unforgettable happening. They have no tradition to follow. In most cases, the client conveys no clearly defined pattern of expectation other than 'surprise us – that's what you're here to do'. The event designer finds himself in a vacuum that combines elements of director, designer, architect, chef, theatre maker and window-dresser. And his creation is, as the organizers of Bread & Butter describe their fashion fair, 'more than just a trade show: it is the mirror of a culture'. Take the opening of the new Louis Vuitton store in Paris. Whimsical projections of light totally transformed the architecture of the leading luxury label's Champs-Élysées façade. Inside – accessible, of course, only to the chosen few – half-naked models were displayed like products on shelves. Adorning the high atrium, another magically illuminated space, was a tableau vivant starring 15 models. Silent and still as statues, they retained their composure among chattering, cocktail-sipping guests. The scene was both surprising and surreal. The designer of this event, Vanessa Beecroft, describes her work as 'filling the gap between art and life, performance and documentary'. Louis Vuitton had previously worked with renowned artists such as Sol Lewitt and Robert Wilson, names that take us remarkably close to the basic principles established by the spiritual father of the happening, Allan Kaprow. Although the main ingredients of the happening (a wide range of creative disciplines) have not changed since the '60s, today's event designers use the latest technologies and the most revolutionary materials. We're surrounded by design 24/7. The whole world has been designed. How can the event designer grab our attention? By creating a new world in which the laws of reality do not apply. By building a 10-m-high illuminated football where potential visitors to the 2006 World Cup in Germany can see soccer-related images projected on rounded walls. By showcasing a Lamborghini, symbol of sophistication, on a bed of nails. It's as though Alice has skidded heels first into the wonderland of the future. Visitors to a travelling exhibition that was put together by the in-house design team of electronics giant Philips can literally step into the future. The latest demonstrators of Philips' cutting-edge products are on show at the exhibition. In line with the current company philosophy, Sense and Simplicity, the Dutch corporation's house of the future has been dubbed Next Simplicity, a title that is illustrated in even the smallest detail of this event. Philips has shown that a successful happening is more than a display of lights, sounds and images. Sometimes it's easier to get people's attention with a veiled whisper than with a piercing shriek. Not a collection of unconnected anecdotes but a coherent story in which each tiny component corresponds to the whole – that is the formula for a successful happening. Nike built a stadium out of sea containers as a setting for a street-football tournament. Graffiti lining the arena replaced the more conventional ads, and goals resembling bent crush barriers replaced the usual post-and-crossbar frames with netting. As rough and unadorned as the street itself, the design conveyed a clear message: street football is a game for everyone. Thus a successful happening is not a self-absorbed spectacle but, on the contrary, an invitation. Come on over. Join in. It can be an unmistakably concrete invitation to participate (get the ball and make the goal), an invitation to pause and ponder, or an invitation to party the night away (no holds barred, anything goes, have a drink and, while you're at it, have a watch as well). The only requirement is you. Without you, it's not an event. And that's precisely what makes it so exciting and special: you make it happen.

Seated guests formed a U-shaped body around the arena in which the fashion show took place. Like makers of modern theatre, the designers experimented with the role of the observers, who ultimately played the part of extras in the performance.

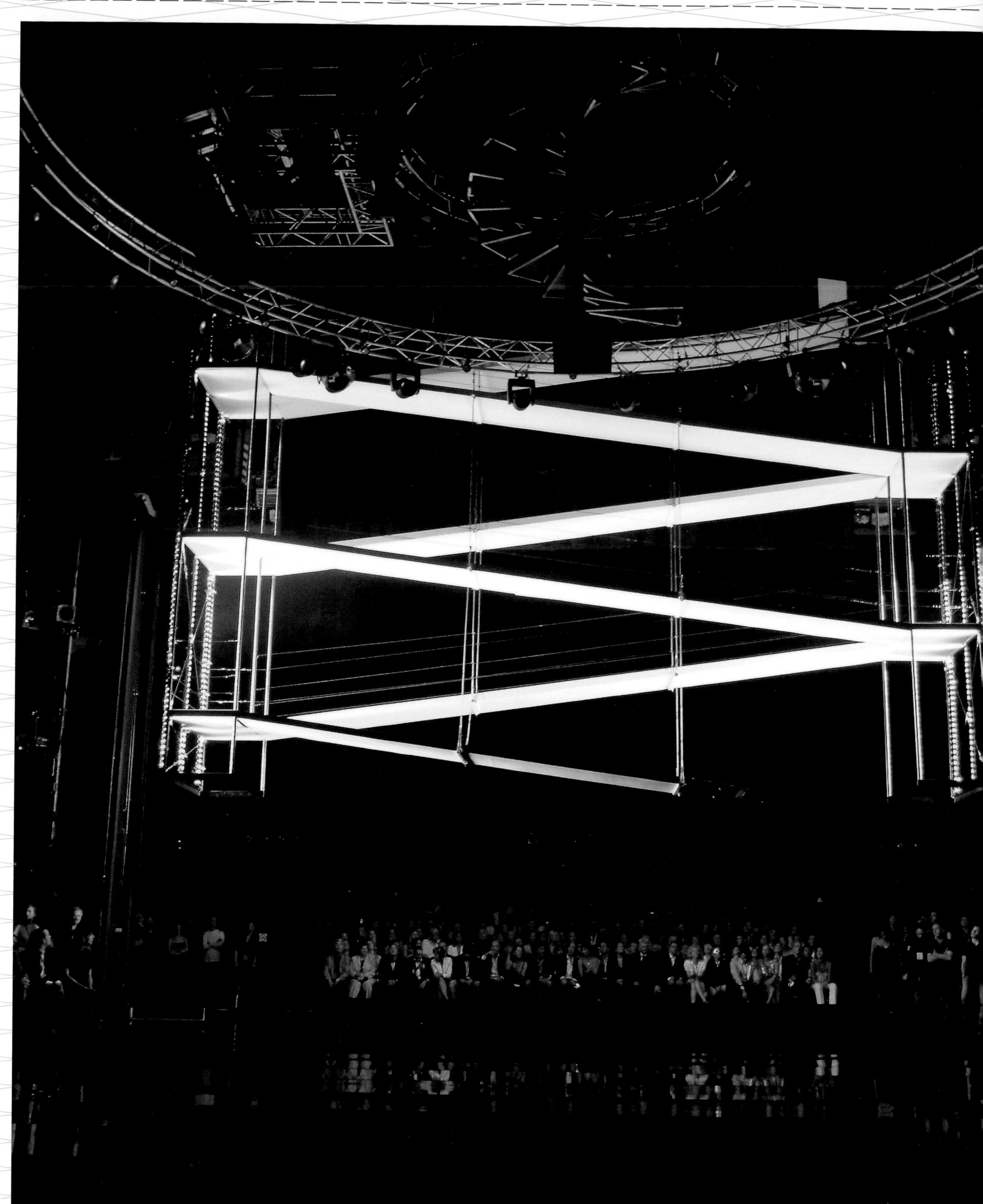

Text by Joeri Bruyninckx

VILLA EUGENIE
HUGO BOSS FASHION SHOW
BERLIN, GERMANY

A Night at the Opera

In the volatile world of fashion, in which countless collections pass in review each year, the so-called 'fashion week' is a traditional high point. It's the place and the moment in which creative talents are launched and established designers confirm their reputations. More than simply a trade-related function that attracts a crowd of designers and buyers, fashion week is an event in which fashion, business and entertainment fuse seamlessly in whatever city is hosting the happening. The brief that German designer Hugo Boss gave to villa eugenie, the agency responsible for staging the new Boss collection during Berlin Fashion Week, was crisp and concise: we want an 'outstanding and surprising' show. And Brussels-based villa eugenie took that message seriously.
Some thousand guests attended the show, which took place on the *Bühne* of the stately German Opera House in Berlin. With this 1600-m^2 stage in mind, the designers, led by Etienne Russo, came up with a remarkable concept based on performances in the capital city's prestigious house of culture. Their idea integrated opera into the fashion show in a surprising manner.
Surprise marked the pageant even before it began, as guests did not enter the building through the foyer, but trickled in through a small back door, from where they were taken on a guided tour of the 'invisible', behind-the-scenes aspect of the opera. Only then did they take their places for the main event – in seats that were arranged, by contrast, on the gigantic, completely empty stage. A backdrop of black velour curtains demarcated the space, veiling the scene in twilit mystery. What's more, the customary catwalk was absent and, in its place, a gleaming black floor filled the arena occupied by the visitors.

The matter-of-factness with which fashion models moved onto the catwalk from an 'island' nearly touching the ceiling revealed the productional precision underpinning the event.

Inspired by the opera, with its scenery changes between acts, Russo and his team took 'a completely different approach' to the conventional fashion show and 'split the show into several acts'. They substituted a subtler type of theatre for the persistent thrust of the more traditional show, which spits out a continuous parade of models strutting to a pulsating beat. When darkness fell like a cloak across the stage and lights came up to reveal the next act, guests were caught in a field of tension and felt the suspense so typical of dramatic opera. The expectant and immediate build-up of excitement culminated in the gradual lowering of a 14-m-high spiral steel staircase, which announced Act I. Models in evening gowns descended the stairs and touched down, nymph-like, on the shiny black floor, clearly echoing the classic operatic performances that inspired the designers.

A set design featuring a single staircase is deceptively simple, an illusion. Here it seemingly ignored the fact that in the eerie gloaming, the element that hung from the high ceiling – the volume that made the production possible – was a structural tour de force: a floating island for about 30 models and back-stage staff. Equally spectacular was the staircase, actually more of a 'footbridge', that appeared at the beginning of Act II. The bridge carefully unfolded to become an 82-m-long walkway and, in so doing, sent the catwalk soaring an extra nine 'tiers' into the air. Special hydraulic motors guaranteed the slow, precise descent of the stairways and ensured the safety of the models, definitely no small task. It was not a show for models with acrophobia.

The set that slid into place for Act III featured a number of gem-like components, their surfaces glittering with 25,000 facets, which optically merged to become a tunnel. The lighting cast bright reflections on floor and backdrop and gave a stunning aura to models emerging from the tunnel. The same majestic setting surrounded the grande finale, in which the models strode, one by one, from the tunnel to stand on a platform in front of VIPS in the first row and receive their applause in the style of a 'theatrical troupe'. At that point, the platform with models and VIPS slowly began to revolve, and the curtains that had separated the stage from the large auditorium throughout the show were drawn to reveal a space filled with enthusiastic opera lovers, who gave a standing ovation not only to the models but also to the astonished guests.

'Not for nothing did we give the show element the working title "Illusion",' says Russo. 'Surprise, appearance and disappearance – that's what the show was about.' Guests who had just been enjoying a theatrical production with no clue of what was awaiting them suddenly became extras in that very performance. In preparing for the event, Russo and his team spent an evening at the opera 'just to see how people behave'. The setting they created suggested that life is a spectacle, that a night out can be a performance, and that fashions by Boss are the perfect props.

'Surprise, appearance and disappearance – that's what the show was about.' Etienne Russo

Designer: villa eugénie – www.villaeugenie.com
Photographers: Xavier Linnenbrink – xavier.linnenbrink@gmail.com
Pepe Botella – p.botella@telefonica.net

Client: Hugo Boss – www.hugoboss.com
Manufacturer: all furniture custom made
Capacity: 2000 guests
Total floor area (m²): 4500
Duration of construction: 7 days
Start of event: 22 July 2005

The spiral staircase appeared to be a perfectly plausible prop for a scene whose players were arrayed in Boss eveningwear. Nightlife so exclusive is obviously bound to make an overwhelming impression.

This page: Bright reflections of light on the gleaming catwalk gave the models a mystically resplendent aura.

'Everything is illusion.' Models seemingly vanished in thin air in a tunnel that was made up of 25,000 reflecting components.

Left, middle and right: Theatrical lighting leading to the fashion show created a play of light and dark, building up tension and filling the room with an air of suspense.

Various Bread & Butter trade-fair stands at the event held in Berlin, July 2006.

S1 ARCHITEKTUR
BREAD & BUTTER
BERLIN, GERMANY AND BARCELONA, SPAIN

Trends on Historical Grounds

Bread & Butter hosts the most world's most influential high-end streetwear; fashion and youth-oriented brands. B&B trade shows are held in Berlin and Barcelona, two fashionable cities rich in youth culture. Apart from the fashions on offer, these events provide a wealth of information and inspiration, while functioning as meeting places for like-minded people and anyone who enjoys the buzz of innovative design. The fairs are like huge parties thrown to add a dash of fun to the business side of fashion.

While running a popular retail establishment with a focus on high-end streetwear and denim, Bread & Butter founder Karl-Heinz Muller found himself constantly on the road in search of the desired variety of cutting-edge brands for his store in Cologne. His decision to bring them all together under one roof in a trade fair targeting retailers led to the first B&B, which took place in 2001. 'For a tasty meal, you need only the essentials: good bread and butter': these words sum up Muller's philosophy with respect to the show. The essentials of B&B are labels that are original, that play a major role in their specific market segment, and that have a distinctive brand identity. What makes the show itself so special is its successful reflection of the world of the target group, including key cultural facets such as architecture, art, music, design and magazines. The concept deviates from that of conventional trade fairs. 'Our approach is less about renting out square metres and more about targeting group-oriented lifestyle concepts.'

Venues are a vital part of Bread & Butter. Rather than presenting fashions in boring, static halls, the organizers have opted for older buildings with character and interesting architecture. The location in Berlin is Kabelwerk, the former Siemens cable factory. Built in 1911, this 55,000-m^2 complex is located on Insel Gartenfeld in Berlin with its industrial charm, a chapter of Berlin's industrial history. It was converted to a trade-fair centre by a local firm, s1 architektur.

Members of Vivienne Westwood's graduating class at UDK (Universitätder Künste, Berlin) showed their fashion designs on the catwalk.

Accommodating the Barcelona show is the historical Fira de Barcelona, home of the World's Fairs of 1929 and the former site of the 1928 Barcelona world exhibition, a fine example of exhibition culture in Europe. Along with being responsible for the redevelopment of Kabelwerk in Berlin and for the master plan of both shows, s1 architektur also oversees the concept.
Metropolises as different as Barcelona and Berlin, both of which have staged successful B&B events, do not compete; they complement each another. Berlin, with its rough-and-ready dynamic, stresses streetwear and a newly honed athletic approach to urban life that epitomizes the northern-European reality, which is clearly distinguishable from that of warm and colourful Barcelona, with its joie de vivre and its equal, if not even stronger, emphasis on sports. The two fairs, both held in July, move to the beat of the fashion industry, kicking off the season's round of shows and bringing together the exciting and innovative themes that are so crucial to today's youth culture, as well as to the retailer's understanding of this ever-changing market. The brands on show – fashions, accessories and other trendsetting products – are inspired by the diversity that marks the society of the young-at-heart.
Exhibitors are as varied as the influences that characterize the events. Hip items and fads are highlighted in themed areas, at stands, at side events and on the heads and bodies of avant-garde visitors to the fair, always a great indicator of what's hot and what's not. Zones with names like 'street culture', 'urban elegance' 'very kids' and 'superior' structure the show and suggest the direction and mood of the season. In Berlin, the Werkstatt zone provides a platform and operates as a recruiting centre and exhibition space for progressive artists, graphic designers, graffiti specialists and the like. This area draws visitors with an interest in aesthetic innovation and in all sorts of new creative concepts. Music and reading material are also very much a part of B&B, and anyone who needs further information on how things are moving in this particular market sector can flip through the huge selection of authoritative international trade and lifestyle magazines that are available at the show.
Although exhibitors are generally responsible for the design of their stands, they do receive guidelines. Walls are normally restricted to a height of 1.60 m, in order to stimulate communication among exhibitors and to give visitors an open, welcome feeling. Both Barcelona and Berlin locations are exceptional and full of history and character. Our urban and architectural concept reflects our sensible approach to each location's specific features. Our aim is to achieve a suspenseful combination of existing structures and temporary constructions.
As the visitor to such an animated event – a place just bursting with activity – it's difficult to imagine the amount of buying and selling that's going on around you, but the figures prove that these fairs have a continuing and growing success. The first show in Cologne attracted 50 exhibitors and 5000 visitors, the show in winter 2006 in Barcelona, 910 exhibitors and 53,774 visitors, from 95 nations. The organizers of Bread & Butter sum it up not only as 'more than just a simple tradeshow', but also as 'the mirror of a culture'.

'More than just a simple tradeshow: it is the mirror of a culture'. Bread & Butter

Designer: s1 Architektur – www.s1architektur.com
Photographer: Bread & Butter – www.breadandbutter.com

Client: Bread & Butter – www.breadandbutter.com
Consultants: Leyendecker, Wink, Daumenkino, Pfadfinderei, Visu Art, Kurvenstar, Schenker, Minga, Viaux, Mehdi Chouakri
Engineer: Corall (Berlin)
Manufacturer: Anina Diener
Floor area (m²): 90,000 (Barcelona), 55,000 (Berlin)
Duration of construction: 2 weeks (Barcelona), 3 - 5 weeks (Berlin)
Start of event: 5 July 2006 (Barcelona), 14 July 2006 (Berlin)

This page: Walls are normally restricted to a height of 1.60 m, in order to stimulate communication among exhibitors and to convey an open, welcome feeling.

Below and bottom: Several spots at the twin trade shows gave visitors an opportunity to sit and relax.

This page and opposite: Panoramic images of various halls at Bread & Butter, the name given to trade shows featuring selected fashion labels and held in Berlin and Barcelona (January 2006).

BARCELONA
DOCKERS

EDDIE PEN

Models arranged in a tableau vivant shared the space with classic pieces of Louis Vuitton luggage.

LOUIS VUITTON
LOUIS VUITTON LAUNCH
PARIS, FRANCE

The Emperor's New Clothes

'Do not speak. Stand still. Be detached. Do not establish direct eye contact. Hold your posture as long as you can. Pretend you are dressed. Pretend no one else is in the room.' Just some of the instructions given to near-naked models at the launch of Louis Vuitton's Champs-Élysées House.

Two performances were held in October 2005 to celebrate the opening of the largest of Louis Vuitton's 352 stores. This particular retail space is part of the architectural heritage of the company, for it was here, on the most famous avenue in the world, that Louis Vuitton commissioned the construction of its first establishment almost a century ago.

Louis Vuitton, a leading luxury label surely unparalleled in terms of style, continues to combine tradition and innovation to create a brand image that is both elegant and contemporary. Founded in 1854, the fashion house has long collaborated with artists and designers to nurture the creativity of its in-house staff. Over the years Louis Vuitton has worked with the likes of Sol Lewitt, César, Takashi Murakami, Robert Wilson and, more recently, James Turrell, Olafur Eliasson and Tim White-Sobieski, whose work enhances the new store. Further reinforcing the creative momentum was the arrival of Marc Jacobs, who joined Louis Vuitton in 1997 as artistic director.

The somewhat daring Champs-Élysées event – the embodiment of Louis Vuitton's spirit of adventure – was the work of artist Vanessa Beecroft, a highly innovative member of a new generation of contemporary artists. Her installations regularly feature groups of young women in uniforms of 'near nudity'. Beecroft describes her work as filling 'the gap between art and life, performance and documentary'. Louis Vuitton, always open to new ideas, gave the artist carte blanche. 'I felt that I could do what I wanted as an artist,' she says, 'and that it was understood by Louis Vuitton.'

Posing in the splendour of the Petit Palais.

Beecroft chose the splendid 20 m-high atrium for the first of the two performances that preceded the official opening of the store. The exclusive event was held for a select group of press-related invitees. Semi-nude models 'wearing' a glowing range of skin tones took strategic positions on shelves displaying classic pieces of luggage selected by Beecroft. The bits of fabric draped and folded on these female bodies reflected classicism and timeless beauty. All 30 models remained on the shelves throughout the presentation, maintaining an absolute absence of human contact. Animation was limited to a barely noticeable shift in posture or the blink of the eye.

The second event was a glittering celebration. A glamorous array of guests enjoyed a cocktail reception at the new store before moving to the beautiful surroundings of the recently renovated Petit Palais, a museum for major art exhibitions that occasionally hosts special fashion shows and similar affairs. On the evening devoted to Louis Vuitton, the Monogram patterns were projected onto the façade of the palace.

Here, again, 15 scantily clad women took their positions in a tableau vivant, standing motionless in the same room with mingling guests who often stopped to gaze at the frozen-in-space scene. No amount of prompting or staring disturbed the composure of the models. Keeping Beecroft's instructions in mind, they did not react or respond to individuals or to anything occurring around them. Beecroft's list of requirements was key to the performance and guaranteed the success of this totally void and dreamlike scene.

Vanessa Beecroft says the secret to her achievement lies in careful preparation. Among other things, she recorded the two-hour live installations on film and, using photography, registered every detail: who's looking, who's being looked at and the reactions of bystanders to the tableau vivant. Initially concerned about staging a retail-related performance, she is glad to have had the opportunity to show her work to a different audience. Guests seemed neither shocked nor surprised but simply enchanted by the sight of surreal arrangements of lovely 'lifeless' feminine forms.

A slightly different opinion was voiced by designer-architect Andrée Putman: 'When it comes to these performances, "ephemeral" is relative… Perhaps what is frightening is (Beecroft's) way of transferring women into beings that aren't really there.' Putman compares the work to 'Freud's "disturbing strangeness" – when a human being becomes a machine or a thing.'

As well as the performances, the artist used the same partially dressed models to create letters of the alphabet. At her studio in New York, the women were arranged in the shape of letters spelling out 'Louis Vuitton' and photographed from above. Beecroft remarks that 'some of the women looked like the pilasters of Italian Renaissance balconies'.

These photographs, along with videos and selected images from the two performances, were exhibited at Espace Louis Vuitton, a light, airy, 400-m² gallery on the seventh floor of the new store, where a panoramic view of the city underpinned Beecroft's awesome art.

Beecroft's list of requirements was key to the performance and guaranteed the success of this totally void and dreamlike scene.

Designer: Louis Vuitton – www.louisvuitton.com
Photographers: J. Cohrssen, V. Knapp, S. Muratet, A. Jarrier and F. Marcellin

Client: Louis Vuitton – www.louisvuitton.com
Consultant: Vanessa Beecroft
Start of event: 12 October 2005

Façade of the Petit Palais, theatrically illuminated with the Louis Vuitton logo.

Below: Models mixed with Louis Vuitton luggage's. Bottom: The soaring central atrium was selected as the site for the first of two performances that paved the way for the official opening of the Champs-Elysées House.

This page: Entrance and interior of the Louis Vuitton Champs-Elysées House in Paris.

An enormous inflated hemisphere became the surreal setting for a Couture Future show.

JEAN BOTTINEAU
COURRÈGES COUTURE SHOW
PARIS, FRANCE

The Courrèges Bubble

On 10 July 2002, an unusual happening took place on a site in central Paris earmarked for Jean Nouvel's Musée du Quai Branly – a bit of prime real estate in the shadow of the Eiffel Tower. The event in question was the Courrèges autumn/winter couture show of 2002/2003, and the venue was a huge futuristic hemisphere that many observers compared to an immense bubble. Courrèges has always been and still is a forerunner in the field of couture – as well as in areas less known to the public. Founded by André Courrèges in 1961, the company is currently in the hands of the effervescent and entrepreneurial Coqueline Courrèges. It was Coqueline Courrèges who realized, while visiting a flat overlooking the building site, that this was the location she had been looking for, a perfect spot for her latest project. But how to get the necessary permission and to implement her plan? With the help of her trusty press officer, Margot Christmann, she managed to persuade everyone involved, allaying all concerns over conditions, security and delays. In the end, the two women even got officials to lend them the bulldozers needed to level the site. When asked about the input of the team at Courrèges, Coqueline Courrèges immediately answers: 'Du courage!' – because she is thoroughly convinced that the project could not have been carried out without courage. She is quick to admit, however, that 'when an idea is crazy, it's usually mine'. Be that as it may, she has a strong and loyal staff that supports her and believes in her. A mere four weeks separated the moment she spotted the site from the day of the show. The structure itself was erected within the space of one week. Her longtime colleague and architect, Jean Bottineau, listened patiently to her ideas – 'as he has done for the past 45 years' –and set to work immediately.

Below: Preparing the entrance to the Couture Future show.
Bottom: A battery-powered car bulle designed by Courrèges drove around the futuristic stage set.

With no time to waste, plans were drawn up, holes were filled, the site was levelled, water and electricity were connected and materials delivered – all in changeable weather conditions. Courrèges had had experience with a similar construction at the Air Air exhibition in Monaco, but that had been an indoor show. Enter ATC, a Brittany-based company that Coqueline Courrèges describes as 'seaman on land'. Normally involved in nautical work, ATC cut and assembled the structure to 'couture standards'. When the gigantic hemisphere had been inflated, it contained a 2000-m^2 space with no walls or columns, an interior soon filled with technical equipment and Bottineau's purpose-designed benches. Environmental issues are extremely important to Courrèges, and over the years staff members have been studying humans and their environment. They used this show to convey their concern about the environmental damage we cause and to suggest possible solutions. They divided their 'message' into four parts, each representing one phase in the history of Courrèges as couturier. One referred to a vision of the future, another to 'air architecture', a third to renewable forms of energy, and the last – the so-called 'second skin' – to an early Courrèges development. Air architecture was demonstrated by the inflatable bubble, which would be deflated and removed from the site within one day after the event had ended. Renewable energy was symbolized by the car *Bulle*, a battery-powered automobile that traces its origins to 1969 but is still awaiting manufacture in its present form. 'We won't commercialize it until we find the best energy,' says an adamant Coqueline Courrèges, implying the use of renewable energy adapted to the big crowd,' says Coqueline Courrèges. 'To reach this goal, 3 prototypes of cars, firstly the *Bulle*, followed by the *EXE*, and the *ZOOOP*, have been constructed in order to improve these new technologies. Car manufacturers are often interested to follow our results.'

'Second skin' is the name of a knitting technique that Courrèges developed in the 1960s and subsequently refined. The latest version is a transparent body stocking that is worn as an undergarment. The company is currently working with scientists to develop new protein-based fibres. Coqueline Courrèges believes that technology and the science of genetics will become vital to the 'couture' industry in the future.

On a beautiful, sunny evening in July 2002, crowds flocked to the bubble, which accommodated 500 people. Taking place in this space-age environment was a circus of events with a message and not simply a fashion show with models parading on the catwalk. It was a happening that attracted a range of visitors, from the fidèle Courrèges devotee to the young woman just about to discover the fashion house and the message behind the clothes.

A few years have passed since the bubble made such a big stir. Revisiting Coqueline Courrèges and her team, we find them still hard at work on sources of renewable energy and busy with the further development of both the electric car and the 'second skin'. The ultimate goal of such dedicated people is to save the earth, and if anyone can do it, it must be Coqueline Courrèges and her entourage.

'When an idea is crazy, it's usually mine.' Coqueline Courrèges

Designer: Jean Bottineau – T + 33 1 5367 3000
Photography: Otto Wollenweber – owollenweber@courreges.com

Client: Courrèges - www.courreges.com
Manufacturer: ATC
Capacity: 500 guests
Total floor area (m2): 2000
Start of event: 10 July 2002

Models taking a bow at the end of the show.

This page: A distinctive collection of fashions by Courrèges lent a sophisticated aura to the event.

This page and opposite: Construction of 'the bubble'; the building site at various stages of completion and in all kinds of weather.

This page: Inspired by the firm's own Nike Laboratories, Nike Brand Design turned Air Celebration into a white-tiled clinical-research lab, complete with benches and sinks.

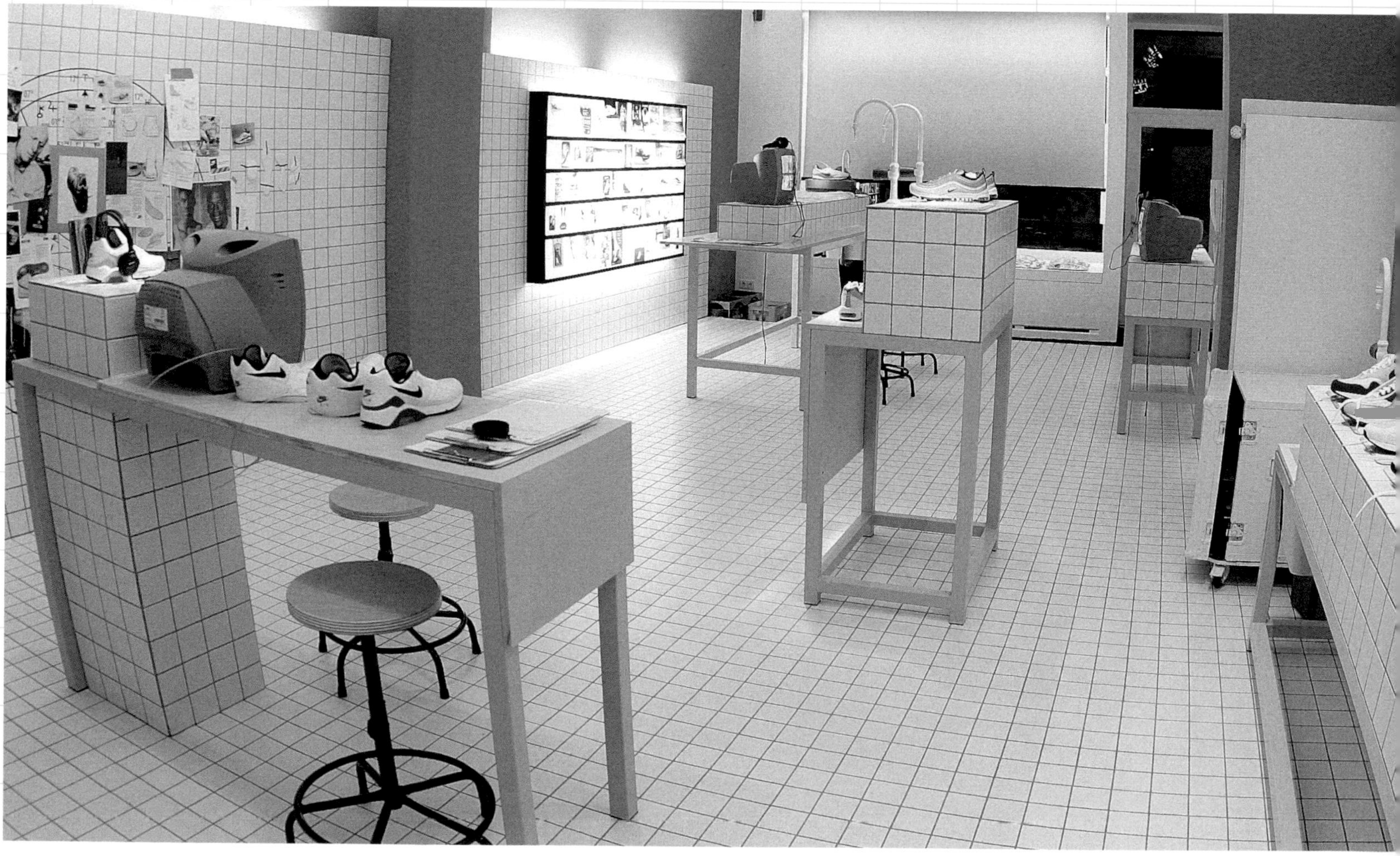

Text by Edwin van Onna

NIKE BRAND DESIGN
AIR CELEBRATION
BERLIN, GERMANY

Walking on Air

Nike Air shoes have become icons of the footwear industry. To celebrate three decades of Nike Air cushioning, Nike Brand Design temporarily transformed a Berlin showroom into a scientific research laboratory dubbed Air Celebration. A mysterious landscape of sketches, prototypes and Air Sole units displayed among sinks, taps, tiles and stools invited visitors to acquaint themselves with the development of Nike Air. Air Celebration also supported the launch of the very latest in trainers: the Air Max 360.
Employing a staff of 30, Nike Brand Design is housed at Nike's European headquarters in Hilversum, The Netherlands. The remaining Brand Design departments, representing the USA and Asia, are located at the firm's American headquarters.
Most Brand Design activities focus on Nike projects such as retail concepts, fixturing systems, media-related events, environments and graphics. 'Not all the work is strictly for Nike,' says Mike Tiedy, creative director of Nike Brand Design. 'Some projects are done with and for our strategic partners, including retailers, sport teams and even individual athletes.'
The Air event was commissioned by Nike Germany. 'The brief from Nike Germany was to create something around the launch and history of Nike Air,' says Tiedy. 'The title was Air Celebration, which Nike Brand Design used as both positioning tool and brief. Nike Brand Design had complete freedom in the process, limited only by budget. Of course, presentations were made to the client to make sure that the event communicated the Air Celebration idea and expectations.'

This page: The uniform white tiling on the walls continues as a surface on components designed as display units.

The Spirit Showroom located in Berlin Mitte is a Nike-run site used for special events and exhibitions. Here artists and designers, among others, are regularly given the opportunity to present their work. The space consists of several offices, an exhibition area, a showroom and a modest Nike iD design pod for customers who want to assemble their own Nike shoes. It was an ideal location for the Air Celebration.

Nike Brand Design transformed the showroom into a clinical laboratory equipped with standard white tiling, research benches, and sinks and taps that could be used to display products. To facilitate dismantlement – the event is scheduled to travel to other locations – the designers mounted the tiles on 'false' walls and floors. According to Tiedy, Nike's reputation as a brand deeply into research inspired the idea of a laboratory as a stage. 'The original idea emerged from Nike laboratories. Nike has had several labs for researching and investigating running, cushioning, kinetics and technology. Although the labs don't really look like the Air Lab in Berlin, the generic laboratory environment creates a symbolic representation of science and technology.'

Nike Brand Design knew exactly what story had to be told. They wanted an event that would clearly convey the technology and history of Nike Air. 'Originally invented in 1979, Nike Air technology has evolved through a series of innovations and patents. Today, the Nike Air 360 has a full-length air sole that provides the most complete cushioning and the most lightweight system from the first step to the last.' They emphasize Nike's desire for innovation, for giving athletes what they need to achieve the best results. 'Nike Air technology is a direct result of Nike's research, which includes communicating with athletes to create better products.' Nike Brand design used several short films and other collateral materials to demonstrate this connection, such as vintage Nike commercials and short interviews with experts who reveal hitherto unknown information about Nike Air technology. The team covered a large wall-mounted light box with ads that exhaustively illustrate the history of Nike Air, from the very first Tailwind to the recent Air 360. Elsewhere, a flip chart displays the chronological development of the shoes. A system of hinged photos enables the visitor to follow this evolution every step of the way.

The initial Air Celebration, which lasted nearly two months, was publicized through invitations, websites, blogs and word-of-mouth advertising. To generate maximum publicity, the event was staged during Bread and Butter, an international fashion fair for up-and-coming labels featuring everything from jeans to 'street couture'. Visitors to the Nike Lounge at the fair were automatically given an invitation to the Spirit Showroom. After its opening in January 2006, Air Celebration welcomed the general public. Staff members working temporarily as guides explained the various exhibits to visitors, pointing out innovations and adding details about the history of Nike Air Technology.

Advertising in the showroom window in Berlin Mitte consisted of a small Nike logo on the glass and a series of eye-catching blue photographs of Air Soles. The images, of different sizes, were arranged to form a rather austere collage. 'The shots of the Air Soles have an X-ray type of look, which helped further the scientific allusion,' says Tiedy. The provocative and somewhat mysterious images are an abstract representation of Nike Air's innovative character. No sports-loving consumer could pass by without noticing them.

'The original idea emerged from a well-known history of Nike laboratories.' Mike Tiedy

Designer: Nike Brand Design – www.nike.com
Photographers: Alex Flach – flach@lodown.com
Vivian van Schagen – vivian.van.schagen@nike.com

Client: Nike Inc. – www.nike.com
Consultant: Nike Brand Design
Manufacturers: Nike Brand Design and Metrofarm
Start of event: January 2006

This page and opposite: Audiovisuals, flip-chart displays and light boxes with photos and advertisements illustrate the historical development of Nike Air Technology.

AIR FORCE 1
CUSHIONING THAT LASTS FOREVER AND EVER
SWOOOOOOOOOOOOOSH.
A REVOLUTION IN MOTION.
THERE'S AIR IN OUR RUNNING SHOES BECAUSE THERE'S NONE IN THE KU'DAMM.
AIR MAX.
MAX
WE SELL SHOES

This page and opposite: Hybrid lab counters with sinks and taps, as well as X-ray images on display windows, emphasize the scientific character of the interior design.

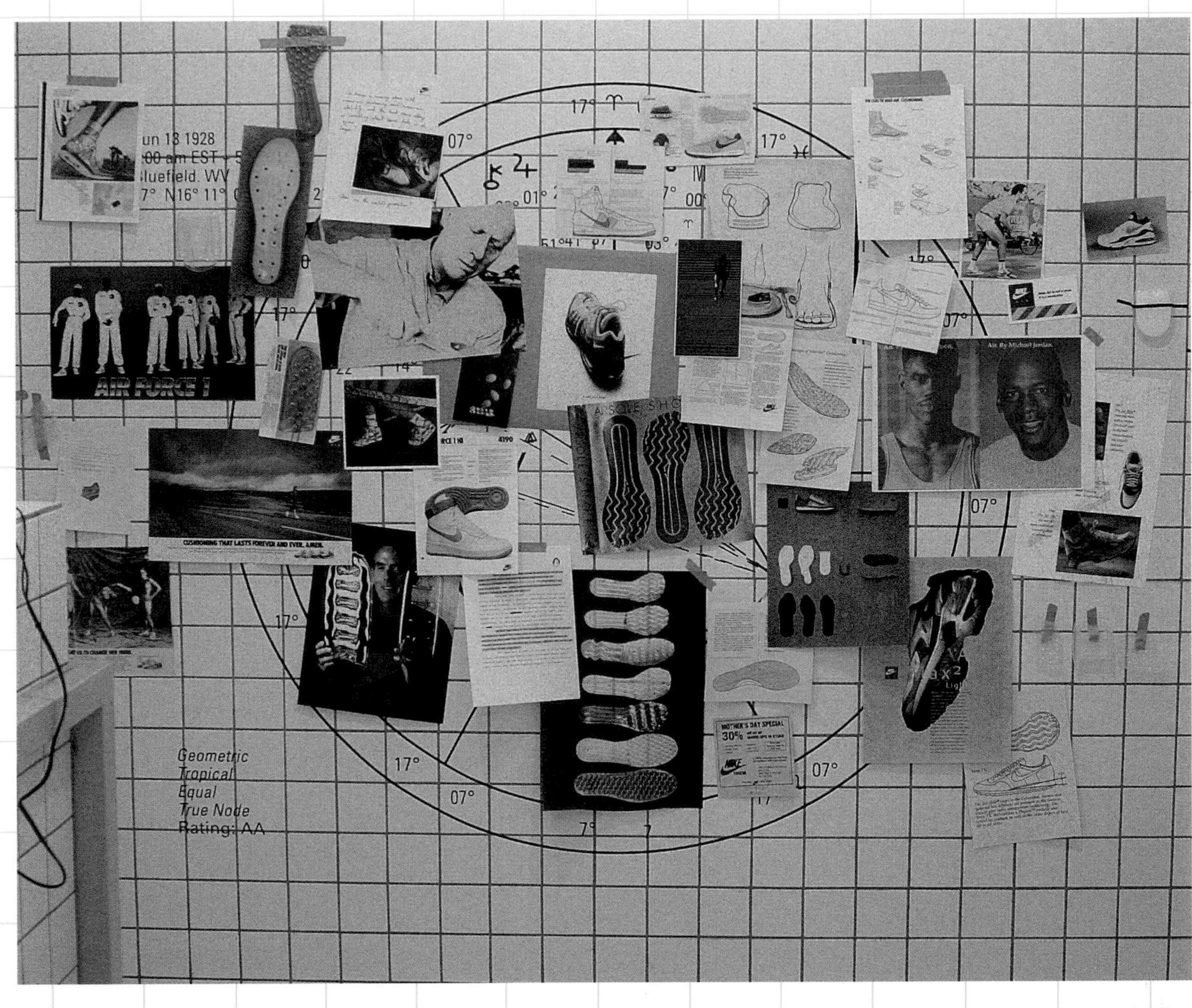
AIR FORCE 1
CUSHIONING THAT LASTS FOREVER AND EVER. AMEN.
MOTHER'S DAY SPECIAL
30%
Geometric
Tropical
Equal
True Node
Rating: AA

Wink upgrades Diesel fashion shows into memorable experiences for international sales teams.

Text by Edwin van Onna

WINK
DIESEL EVENTS

A Show for All Seasons

Dutch event-planning firm Wink 'dresses' the fashion shows for international sales teams allied with Italian jeans brand Diesel. Wink's seasonal sets enhance locations as diverse as an Olympic football pitch and a site high in the hills of Crete. The backdrop is a striking element of the show, but work by Wink transcends the design of props. From start to finish, Wink provides a memorable 'brand experience' that gives sales managers a clear idea of what inspires Diesel designs.

Wink specializes in the art direction of shows, raves, festivals, trade-fair stands, meetings and such. The company develops concepts and produces, manages and realizes events. Projects include festivals such as Bacardi Bat Beats, Bread and Butter, Drum Rhythm, The Higher Ground (Lowlands), Elle Style Event, Coke: feel1vibe, and the North Sea Jazz Festival. Wink's origins in the dance scene help the designers to see 'the event' as the ultimate multimedia immersion: a well-planned event provides a wow experience. 'Wink's background gives the outfit an edge on the competition', says creative director Arne Koefoed. 'Dance events have a fast, interactive quality that's heightened by lighting, special effects and video. The live character lends itself to rapid shifts in the overall production, which makes for a high level of synergy and creates room for improvisation.' Big events are ideal platforms for spectacles like laser shows, fireworks and LED displays.

With such images in mind, Diesel creative director Wilbert Das contacted Wink. 'He wanted to shake up Diesel's in-house product presentations,' says Koefoed. 'He felt that the younger generation of salespeople knew too little about the original character of the brand. Even without a specific brief, we came up with a wild plan that was so well received that Das invited us to the head office in Molvena.'

This page: For the 2005 Diesel Futuropolis show, Wink designed an inflatable catwalk and installed it at a unique, hand-picked location: a peak on the island of Crete.

Designer: Wink – www.welcometowink.nl
Photographers:
Airworks – www.airworks.nl
Decodel – info@decodel.nl
Giannoni Giovanni Fotografo – giannonigiovanni@libero.it

Client: Diesel – www.diesel.com

Event: Futuropolis
Location: Aghia Pelagia, Crete
Capacity: 350
Total floor area (m²): 500
Duration of construction: 3 days
Start of event: 12 June 2004

Event: Wild Wild East
Location: Bread and Butter hall, Germany
Capacity: 600
Total floor area (m²): 4000
Duration of construction: 3 days
Start of event: 5 December 2004

Event: Live 25
Location: Bassano del Grappa, Italy
Capacity: 45.000
Total floor area (m²): 50.000
Duration of construction: 5 days
Start of event: 5 September 2004

Event: Dieseldorf
Location: Düsseldorf, Germany
Capacity: 300
Total floor area (m²): 2000
Duration of construction: 2 days
Start of event: August 2004

Event: Trash Your Island
Location: Marbella, Spain
Capacity: 300
Total floor area (m²): 1500
Duration of construction: 2 days
Start of event: 10 June 2003

In recent years Wink has organized the shows and after parties for international sales meetings at which Diesel presents the latest campaigns, websites, retail ideas and marketing concepts. Wink is also responsible for parties and presentations for Diesel Benelux and Diesel Germany; briefs for these events come from the marketing department in question. International sales meetings, however, are collaborative affairs that include Wink, the creative team in Molvena, and event manager GianFranco Fina. 'Fina and his team find a location that satisfies Diesel's requirements concerning hotel and conference rooms. My partner, Bart Bruinsma, and I then visit the place to determine the best spot for the show,' says Koefoed. 'Meanwhile, we're looking at mood boards and graphics to get a feel for the coming collection, which won't be retailed for more than a year. Last summer in Thessaloniki, we found a football pitch close to the hotel – a space suitable for showing the 2006 Spring/Summer collection.' Line Release SS'06, the collection in question, was influenced by Asian folklore and 1940s militarism. The setting was a grandstand made from stone, which allowed Wink to end the event with a dazzling display of fireworks. Wink transformed the grandstand into an oriental temple equipped with a catwalk shaped like a golden dragon. Light effects and musical performances quite literally set the place on fire.
Wink has been working with Diesel since 1999. In spring 2003 they did the Trash Your Island show in Marbella. Eye-catcher there was a stunning catwalk with a graphic backdrop of LEDs and a volcano spewing bubbles, fire, light and smoke. Inspiration was Diesel's 2004 Spring/Summer collection, which featured pirates, buccaneers and 'tropical trash'. Coloured sand and side walls adorned with raffia highlighted the serpentine catwalk. Different but equally surprising was Diesel Futuropolis on Crete a year later, a show based on Brazil, sci-fi and Utopia. Models strode down an immense, inflatable, five-armed catwalk crowned with a globe 8 metres in diameter. Spicing up the futuristic design were Brazilian carnival dancers, a Ziggy Stardust performance and a laser show.
Wink works on its projects for Diesel with a regular team of specialists and freelancers, including Joost van Bellen and Sander Stenger (music), Koen Peeters (lighting design), and Johan Manschot of Echt! (multicultural graphic design). When the concept for the show has been determined, they bring in set builders, VJs, performers and special-effects experts.
Close cooperation between Wink and Diesel's graphic designers is vital. 'They give us tangible examples of ideas that gave rise to current collection,' says Koefoed. A good example is Wild Wild East, a sales meeting in Berlin for the presentation of the 2005 Autumn/Winter collection. The entire setting was based on clothes that fused American and Russian folklore. Wink applied Russian prints to a jumbo, diesel-powered truck made in USA, and designer Johan Manschot blew up Diesel graphics to 'event scale'. The truck made a sensational entrance into the hall, pulling a 30-m-long catwalk. Models emerged from the centre of an enormous 'Russian' sheriff's badge. A classic Wild Wild Wink experience.

A well-planned event provides a wow experience.

This page and opposite: American and Russian folklore got together at Wild Wild East, a sales meeting in Berlin that featured a gigantic customized diesel truck towing a 30-m-long catwalk.

ТОЛЬКО ДЛЯ СМЕЛЫХ

This page: Wink turns each fashion event into a brand experience that gives sales managers an insight into the inspiration behind Diesel designs.

This page: Graphic backdrops paired with spectacular LED-illuminated light shows reveal the roots of Wink, a Dutch event-planning firm with a reputation for organizing dance events.

Left and right: The adidas press release couples Stella McCartney's sleek winter sportswear with a 'must-have attitude'.

ADIDAS AND GAINSBURY AND WHITING
ADIDAS BY STELLA MCCARTNEY
ASPEN, COLORADO, USA

Sweat and Be Beautiful

It was an eye-catching event. Lithe beauties coolly performed their yoga exercises – not in a peaceful yoga centre, but in the middle of SoHo, with traffic roaring by and passers-by stopping to admire the scenery. Large transparent-plastic cubes provided sufficient calm in front of the New York adidas store. Like glass domes, they sheltered the models from the hurly-burly of 136 Wooster Street. A German sportswear manufacturer from Herzogenaurach used this guerrilla marketing tactic to advertise its spring collection: adidas by Stella McCartney.
It all began with a sneaker. As early as 2002, Stella McCartney had collaborated with adidas in designing a sneaker for one of her fashion shows. Subsequently, the Bavarian company commissioned the fashion designer and daughter of Beatle Paul McCartney to design for adidas. In September 2004, Stella McCartney and adidas presented their first Sport Performance Design Collection for Women. The graduate of London's Central St Martins College of Art and Design, now a VIP of fashion, was well on her way to putting together a genuine sports line. Adidas by Stella McCartney is not a streetwear collection, however. These keep-fit fashions fall into the category of functional sportswear. Well known for her seductive feminine creations, McCartney apparently saw something seriously lacking in the sportswear available to women. Those who didn't want to jog and work out in XS men's gear or garish pink and yellow outfits had virtually no alternatives.

Below: A winter wonderland in Aspen, Colorado, was the perfect backdrop for the launch of Stella McCartney's adidas collection for women.
Bottom: Pirouette in the enchanted forest.

In March 2006, the successful collaboration between adidas and McCartney was extended to 2010. At the moment, new collections are introduced twice a year and sold in select stores. Once a male-oriented firm strongly associated with soccer, adidas likes the idea of appealing directly to women. 'The market has a huge demand for stylish sportswear for women,' says McCartney. 'In today's world, women should not have to compromise between style and performance.' Aesthetics and functionality are not incompatible. According to McCartney, women not only want to sweat but also to look good. Keep-fit fashions bearing the 34-year-old designer's signature are made from high-tech fabrics. Garments featuring atypical feminine cuts, muted earthy colours, and details such as gathers and Velcro fasteners look nothing like the usual turn-of-the-century sportswear for women. Adidas-McCartney collections include products for running, gym, tennis and swim.

Of course, clothes for other types of sport are on the drawing board as well. As we go to press, the spotlight is on McCartney's winter sportswear for the 2006 Autumn/Winter Collection. Ignoring New York and London, adidas chose a special venue, some 3000 m above sea level, for the fashion show. Guests were invited to Aspen, Colorado, 'a place which is intimately linked with winter sports, style and design', according to Nelly Kennedy, Global Head of adidas Lifestyle Brand PR. Hand-picked female Lifestyle editors from all over the world came to the rustically luxurious Elk Mountain Lodge, a highlight of the glitzy Rocky Mountain village, to enjoy the lavish presentation, which, says Kennedy, was developed in-house as an event that reflected the fusion of Performance and Style and was nothing like 'a classic fashion show'. Adidas replaced the traditional catwalk with athletes in action: a cast of experienced women skiers, snowboarders and runners. 'We are serious about what we say,' says Kennedy, stressing that 'outfits for professionals, such as the Top 20 Tennis player Maria Kirilenko, are exactly the same as for amateurs'.

In an eight-minute show staged at dusk in front of the lodge, an event organized in collaboration with London production agency Gainsbury and Whiting, athletes wearing McCartney's practical, high-tech fashions – including a one-piece ski suit, quilted jackets and an ingenious running shoe – displayed their talents for the assembled guests.

'The collection is multifaceted and strong on ensembles,' says Kennedy. 'That's why we wanted to present a variety of sports.' The show featured athletes running on a snow-covered jogging track, ice skaters pirouetting on a small ice rink, snowboarders showing off their stunts, and a husky-drawn sled – the 'logo' of the collection – transporting the 'models'.

Guests viewed the spectacle in comfort from two snowy terraces, the upper of which was a snug, inviting space with fireplace, where snowwomen sported accessories from the new collection. Kennedy calls the scene below 'a kind of magical forest'. Contributing to the intimate atmosphere was a lighting scheme that combined light chains, lanterns and spotlights. Instead of the latest chart hits, a background of '80s tunes, such as ' Ice, ice baby', cleverly referred to the theme of the presentation as well as Stella McCartney's parentage. The launch set a high standard. Hold your breath as Germany and England prepare for their next match!

Adidas replaced the traditional catwalk with athletes in action: a cast of experienced women skiers, snowboarders and runners.

Concept: Nelly Kennedy, adidas – www.adidas.de
Production: Gainsbury & Whiting, London – www.gainsburyandwhiting.com
Photographer: Ben Allen – www.focus-photography.net

Client: adidas by Stella McCartney – www.adidas.com/stellamccartney
Duration of event: 2 days
Start of event: 20 March 2006

Sportswomen in action: The stylish presentation of McCartney's sportswear collection took place in a snowy setting in front of Aspen's Elk Mountain Lodge.

stella McCartney

This page: Taking the place of a catwalk
were a skating rink and a snow-covered jogging track.

Below: Stella McCartney explains the concept of her new collection.
Bottom: A quilted ski jacket offers the wearer beautiful protection from the cold.

In the lobby, seating clusters – each composed of four stools and one armchair – formed 'suites' for journalists and celebrities.

TOTEMS COMMUNICATION & ARCHITECTURE
MOMENTS OF SKIN / MILAN FASHION WEEK
MILAN, ITALY

Far More Than Skin Deep

Four times a year, Milan plays host to the fashion world. During the city's so-called Fashion Weeks the shows, highlighted by Milano Moda Donna, are closely watched internationally, as designs seen here set the trends for the coming season. Besides the many events held inside and outside the mid-city exhibition centre, several trade fairs take place as well. Clustered around one of the major catwalks in early 2006 were corporate sponsors of Fashion Week promoter Camera Nazonale della Moda Italiana. Included in the group was P&G Beauty, a branch of Procter & Gamble, which is dealing with beauty products. A growing multinational business with more than 102,000 employees in over 80 countries, P&G makes and markets consumer goods. Among its recent acquisitions are Gillette and Braun. Even earlier, P&G Beauty had taken over Wella, a manufacturer of hair-care projects with headquarters in Darmstadt. Before joining the P&G family, Wella had commissioned Totems Communication & Architecture to carry out several projects. Rather than being ignored by P&G after the takeover, Totems' past work led to a call from Geneva, where P&G has its European headquarters. The people at P&G wanted Totems to develop a modular, multipurpose concept for a 150-m^2 space that was to serve as a meeting place for journalists and fashion designers in Milan. Totems suggested a two-day workshop with other participants in Geneva. Totems accepted the commission. Totems explains they aren't often the recipient of such a straightforward proposal – not that we weren't pleased with the phone call. The firm's preferred practice, and the one most often followed, is to develop a concept together with the client through goal-oriented discussions on practical issues. Totems says they appreciated the absence of a content-related brief before the workshop started, as well as the opportunity to develop the design with five other participants.

Below: First rule for beautiful skin: a peaceful and stress-free environment.
Bottom: The space served as a meeting place for journalists and fashion designers.

P&G beauty

Totems works in close collaboration with a Dutch trend-analist. In the early stages of the P&G project, they analysed the group to be targeted at the trade fair: professional journalists and fashion designers presumed to be candid, self-confident individuals. The next step was to create an environment in which both groups would feel comfortable – a public place that would nonetheless allow visitors to meet and talk in relatively quiet surroundings. Those attending the workshops were not informed of the exact location of the stand, but they were given the approximate dimensions and told that it would be a three-sided space within a row of other stands.

As a branch of Procter and Gamble and an umbrella organization responsible for a wide range of brands, P&G Beauty needed a core image. P&G's public-relations representative, who attended the workshops, had a simple icon in mind, a symbol that would convey the company's core activity: the development and marketing of skin-care products.

The designers chose 'skin' as a basic theme for further elaboration. They saw it as a concept that could be realized spatially and that would appeal to visitors in a sensuous way. Drawing an obvious comparison between 'skin' and 'membrane', Totems says that 'skin envelops the body and is elastic'.

As a number of P&G beauty products not only interact with current fashion trends but also offer high-tech treatments that interact with the top layer of the skin and promise a more youthful look, workshop participants used the skin and its various layers as the foundation of their design concept.

The result was an elastic membrane composed of three layers that together formed a fusion of fashion, skin and technology. To complement the theme of the membrane, they designed freestanding modular furniture to be arranged in the space, including a floor-to-ceiling showcase that partitioned off the service area visually and functionally, while also displaying a selection of P&G skin-care products.

In the lobby, clusters of seating encircled a central platform designed for interviews with celebrities and journalists. All parties agreed that the choice of materials should be geared to current trends, a decision they hoped would flatter the international arbiters of taste.

The outcome of their work was a space that included white-stained, oak-veneered walls; slate-clad shelving; a gleaming membrane made from fabric, woven aluminium and, sandwiched between them, an elasticized material printed with dots to resemble the pores of human skin. Coloured light rippled over the surface of the membrane, which featured the same weave as the layer in the middle. This colour changing gave you the same feeling as a healthy blush on the cheeks. Completing the scene were flat screens set into one wall – monitors that silently transmitted TV adverts for the various brands – and the sounds of calm electronic background music installed to soothe and entice.

P&G's public-relations representative had a simple icon in mind, a symbol that would convey the company's core activity.

Designer: Totems Communication & Architecture – www.totems.com
Photographer: Lulu Poletti – lulupoletti@hotmail.com

Client: Procter & Gamble – www.pg.com
Multimedia consultant: Procon Event Engineering
Manufacturer: mac messe- und ausstellungscenter Service
Capacity: 70 guests
Total floor area (m²): 150
Duration of construction: 4 days
Start of event: 18 February 2006

This page and opposite: Totems' elastic membrane composed of three layers together formed a fusion of fashion, skin and technology.

This page and opposite: A stage for the stars of the P&G Beauty ensemble.

A touring exhibition entitled Next Simplicity lets guests experience the advantages of what Philips Electronics calls 'simplicity-led design'.

Text by Edwin van Onna

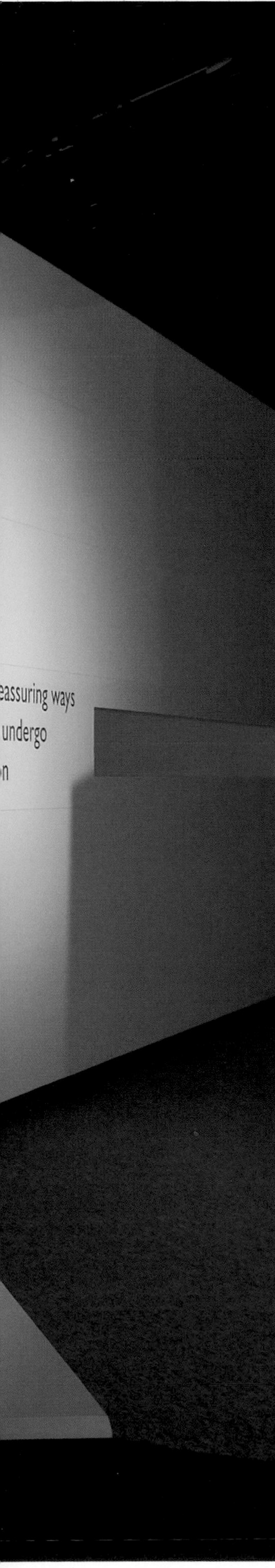

PHILIPS DESIGN
NEXT SIMPLICITY

Tomorrow Made Tangible

Having introduced its new brand promise – Sense and Simplicity – Philips turned to design to explore tangible yet inspirational ways of communicating these three words through 'simplicity-led design'. The solution, created by Philips Design, is Next Simplicity, a project that conveys the company's vision of simplicity, while focusing on technological innovations, sociological trends and, above all, benefits to the user. The designers developed innovative concepts and working models around five themes: care, glow, play, share and trust. Highlighting the exhibits is ease of use. To bring the vision to life, Philips invited relevant stakeholders to experience Sense and Simplicity at a number of Simplicity events. And Next Simplicity concepts were incorporated into an exhibition as part of a greater Simplicity event that travels the world. The event comprises five islands in three 'business focus' areas: health care, lifestyle and technology. Conveying the Sense and Simplicity offered by these concepts are actors who demonstrate how each concept works, explain the thought behind the concept and show how it can benefit the user.
The exhibition guides visitors past designs that, theoretically, could be brought to market after three to five years of further development. Because many of the concepts are based on light and/or sound, the islands have to be well separated from one another. Philips Design opted for enclosed islands with individual floor plans, each geared to the experience in question. 'The settings are fairly neutral,' says Yasushi Kusume, vice president of Philips Design. 'We didn't try to build a real garden, kitchen or living room – what we created are abstract representations.'

This page: Each pavilion is designed as an abstract representation of a kitchen, a living room, a garden and so forth.

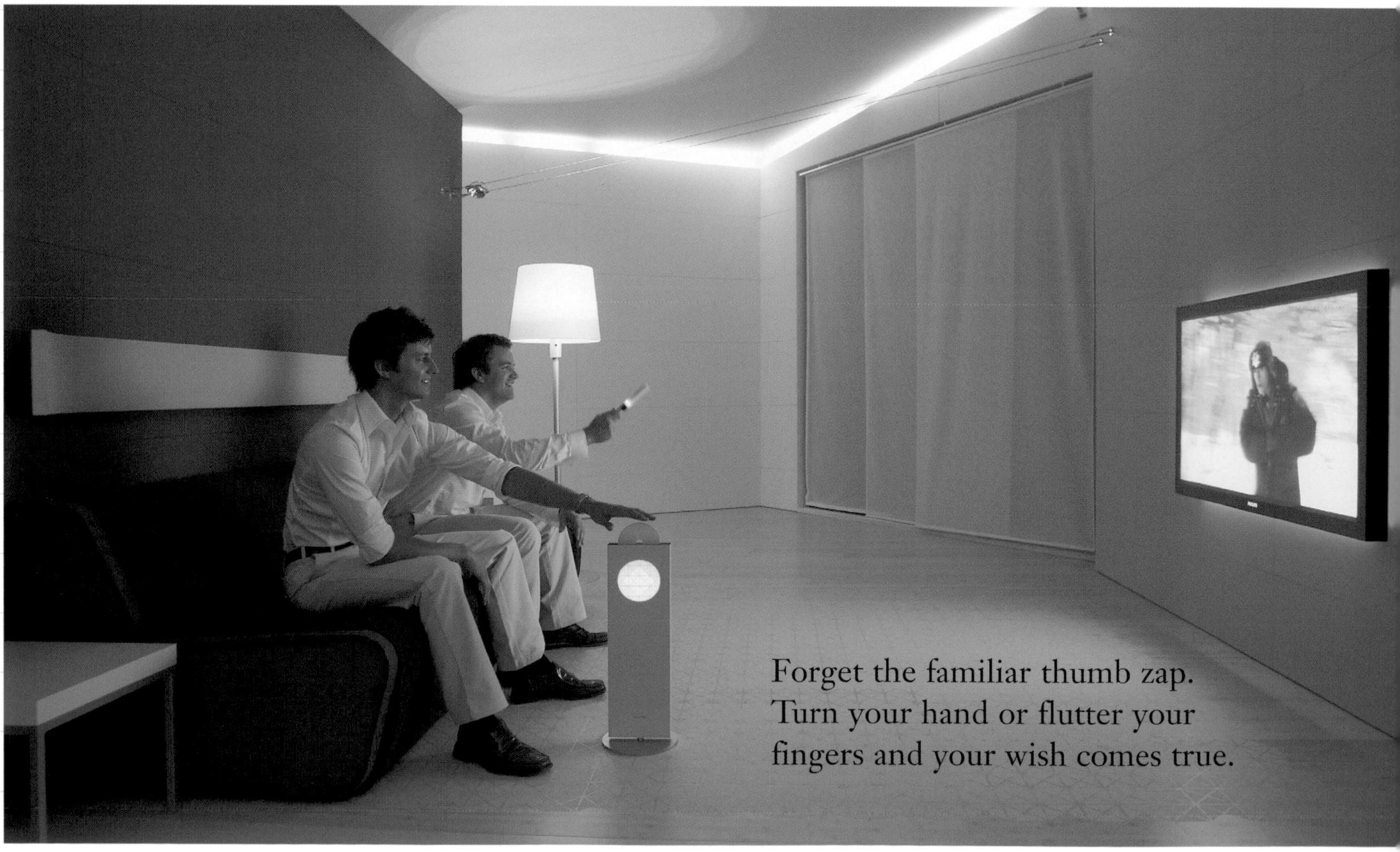

Forget the familiar thumb zap. Turn your hand or flutter your fingers and your wish comes true.

The idea behind the exhibition is to share hypothetical concepts with customers, business partners, opinion leaders, the design community and the media. 'Next Simplicity is our way of communicating hypothetical suggestions,' says Kusume. 'It's a sort of market review of future scenarios. We're not showing fully specified prototypes but concepts that demonstrate key functions, to clarify what we want to communicate.'

Interaction is vital to the demonstration of Sense and Simplicity. In the case of Glow, which encompasses new lighting concepts, the exhibition presents LEDs that change colour at the wave of a hand and a floor lamp, Chameleon, with an integrated scanner that 'picks up' the colour of a scanned object and transfers it to the lamp. The ease of a simple gesture to activate a 'demonstrator' is presented at other islands as well. Visitors to Play are introduced to the Illusion system, which features a TV with a remote control that works like a magic wand. Forget the familiar thumb zap. Turn your hand or flutter your fingers and your wish comes true.

Next Simplicity may offer a glimpse of advanced technology, but it begins with an understanding of a targeted audience. A major objective is to ensure that Philips' visionary products represent simplicity to such groups. 'We're mainly feeding people's imaginations. Our hypothetical solutions are a way to get a reaction and relevant feedback from them. What's missing? Any better ideas? Is this what you're looking for? This feedback enriches our "people research" data. We interview people, and we trace their reactions to the exhibition via weblogs.' It's an approach typical of Philips Design, an organization that's focused on innovation, trend analysis, 'people research', sustainable design and image creation – areas of design that have proved interesting not only to Philips but also to other firms.

In recent years, Philips Design has used its expertise in developing innovative concepts to advise clients other than Philips. This collaborative approach benefits all involved. A diversity of activities broadens the experience and capabilities of Philips Design, allows the team to make new connections, and results in even better insights into innovation for clients. It's an excellent example of multi-partner reciprocity. Philips Design's wide range of customers includes Ford, Nike, Microsoft, P&G, Orange, Bosch, IBM, Unilever and Microsoft.

Next Simplicity opened at the first Simplicity event in September 2005 at L'Espace Grande Arche in Paris before travelling to Amsterdam and New York. The final stop for 2006 is London. One criterion for selecting locations is the placement of islands. 'The ideal layout for the islands is circular, within one space,' says Kusume. 'This allows for an uninterrupted flow from island to island. At one island, we project images onto the ceiling, making it necessary to choose a space with enough height.'

Next Simplicity differs from an ordinary exhibition or trade-fair stand. Invitation-only guests are guided through the space, theme by theme, in select groups of about 20 at a time. At each island they view the exhibits, listen to the information presented and 'experience' the concepts. Ten minutes later, they move to the following island. The programmed tour allows full experience of each island. 'The demonstrators and exhibitions are extremely vulnerable,' says Kusume. 'Letting people wander around unsupervised is too risky.'

Next Simplicity also gives company personnel an insight into Philips's all-in-one philosophy. 'For our employees, the exhibition is tangible evidence of the One Philips Promise,' says Kusume. 'It gives us something concrete to go on, something we can be proud of.' He sees an advantage in the ability of this medium to present and communicate a broad-based company vision. 'We can't do that at a trade fair, which is invariably limited to one product sector. Showing lighting and medical concepts at CeBit, for example, is not an option. Next Simplicity permits us to present ourselves as a brand.'

Designer: Philips Design – www.design.philips.com
Photographer: Philips Design – www.design.philips.com

Client: Philips Design – www.design.philips.com
Engineers: Philips Applied Technology and Philips Solid State Lighting
Manufacturers: Bruns, Kemo, MST, Rena and Tim
Capacity: 100 guests
Total floor area (m²): 322
Duration of construction: 5 days
Start of event: September 2005

This page and opposite: Guests are led through five thematic islands, or 'wonder rooms', which form a circle in most of the locations selected for the exhibition.

PHILIPS
PHILIPS
sense and simplicity
trust
PHILIPS
play

This page and opposite: Hypothetical interactive products demonstrated in the Next Simplicity islands test the imagination of guests and, in most cases, get a response.

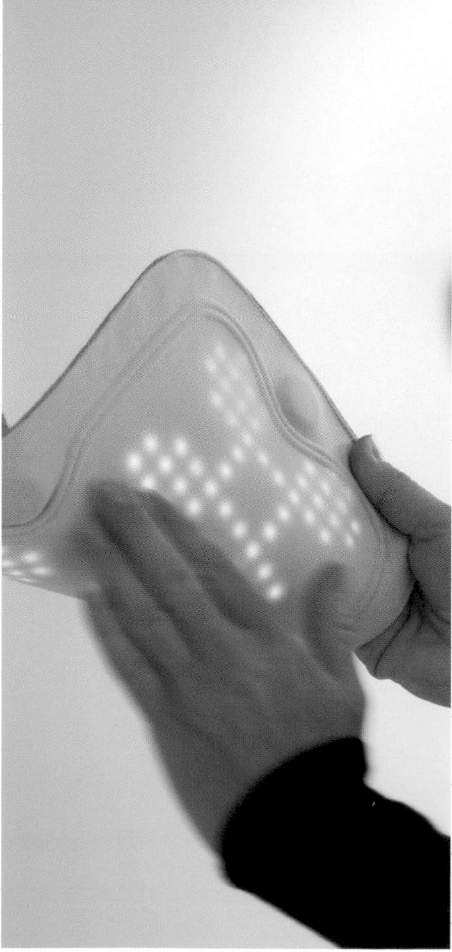

Reduced to an icon: the British Embassy in Berlin becomes a party pavilion.

DASPROJEKT
125 YEARS BILFINGER BERGER
MANNHEIM, GERMANY

A City Built for Celebrations

The success of Bilfinger Berger, a construction company going global with 50,000 employees worldwide, which meanwhile advanced to a Multi Service Group with its corporate headquarters in Mannheim, is based on a longtime tradition in the handling of construction and providing operational services.
In June 2005 Bilfinger Berger celebrated its 125th anniversary. On the Maimarkt, an exhibition area just outside the city gates, a temporary 7000-m^2 'Bilfinger Berger City' was erected for several anniversary celebrations. DasProjekt, a young architecture and interior-design outfit from Hofheim am Taunus, led by Rolf Pauw and Carsten Schmidt, took on the architectural design of the event. Event-planning agency Voss + Fischer, hired by Bilfinger Berger to develop the concept and organize the celebrations, selected DasProjekt to help with the job. 'It was love at first sight,' laughs Pauw. 'The collaboration went wonderfully well. The agency already had a concept for the event, but no idea how it could be realized spatially. That's where we came in.'
A three-dimensional plan of an imaginary city framed the events. 'Our aim was to document and to present the various spheres of activity of our clients in an entertaining way,' explains Pauw, adding that Voss + Fischer had already chosen a palette of bright, strong colours and that all graphics for the event were to be done by a graphic-design team. 'But we were responsible for everything to do with architecture.'
According to Pauw, the greatest challenge was the ground plan. The layout had to include an event area with a stage, enough space for a diversity of exemplary projects, and room for ample seating, tables, bar areas and so forth. 'We drew the layout for the roads and then added the buildings,' says Schmidt, who calls the evolution of the city 'an extrusion of the two-dimensional ground plan'.

This page: A surface of tarmac painted in gaudy colours formed the leitmotif of Bilfinger Berger City.

Pauw and Schmidt covered over two thirds of the area with a 4500-m², open-sided Delta tent. At the entrance, visitors were met by the so-called Wall of Fame. This installation, which was made out of curved partitions up to 5 m high, flanked both sides of a meandering path and displayed the history of the firm.

The Wall of Fame was a prelude to the main event area, which occupied a 500-m² piazza, similar to a market square, at the end of the winding path. In contrast to the curvaceous walls, the plan of the piazza was orthogonal. In line with the entrance was a stage with a rear wall illuminated by LEDs, which formed the focal point. A large area fronting the stage provided the public with tables and chairs. DasProjekt custom-designed the boxlike, grey bars and counters that were spread across the piazza. 'We even supervised the floral decoration on the counters to ensure that they matched the overall concept,' says Pauw. The analogy of the city continued in the form of 'buildings' surrounding the piazza and the network of streets that connected them. A number of grey cubes, the tallest of which was 5.5 m, accommodated cloakrooms, toilets and backstage facilities. An additional seven structures were models of Bilfinger Berger's core projects. On one side of the square stood a simplified version of the Svinesund Bridge, which links Sweden and Norway. On the other was the Nigerian Abuja Stadium, and next to the stage stood the Alte Oper of Frankfurt. Accompanying each project were relevant details printed on the exterior of the buildings and an audiovisual presentation inside.

Pauw compares the construction of the exhibition site to that of a trade fair. 'The project allowed us to apply all our architectural expertise. A major problem was wind, however. The site was close to the airport, and partition walls, being very light, had to be well tethered. Before the event, a structural engineer checked to make sure everything was secure.'

The amount invested in this short-lived event is visible particularly in the 'floor' used throughout Bilfinger Berger City. 'Originally, there was gravel everywhere, making it impossible for us to erect structurally sound buildings,' says Schmidt. 'Wooden flooring was out of the question, because of warping. We covered the entire area in tarmac especially for the event, and a road-marking company gave it a glossy surface. The city had to stand up to some 2000 visitors. The tarmac was removed after the event was over.'

DasProjekt spent a good six months working on the architecture for thc jubilee celebrations. Building the city took a month, the celebrations three days and dismantlement just one night. 'That's how event architecture is,' says Pauw laconically. 'It's a fleeting business.'

'Building the city took a month, the celebrations three days and the dismantlement just one night.' Rolf Pauw

Idea/concept: Voss + Fischer - www.voss-fischer.de
Architecture: DasProjekt – www.atelier-dasprojekt.de
Photographer: Voss + Fischer – www.voss-fischer.de

Client: Bilfinger Berger
Lighting consultant: Neumann & Müller
Graphic consultant: desres design group
Multimedia consultants: Neumann & Müller
Manufacturers: De Boer, Susannah Martin Backdrops, Zeeh Design Messebau
Capacity: 2500 guests
Total floor area (m²): 4500 (tent), 2500 (outdoor area)
Duration of construction: 4 weeks
Start of event: 24 June 2005

A stage, a bar and a landmark: everything needed to create an urban piazza.

Bilfinger Berger
Dienstleistungen
Services

This page and opposite: Fade to grey: all architectural elements of the city sported the colour of concrete.

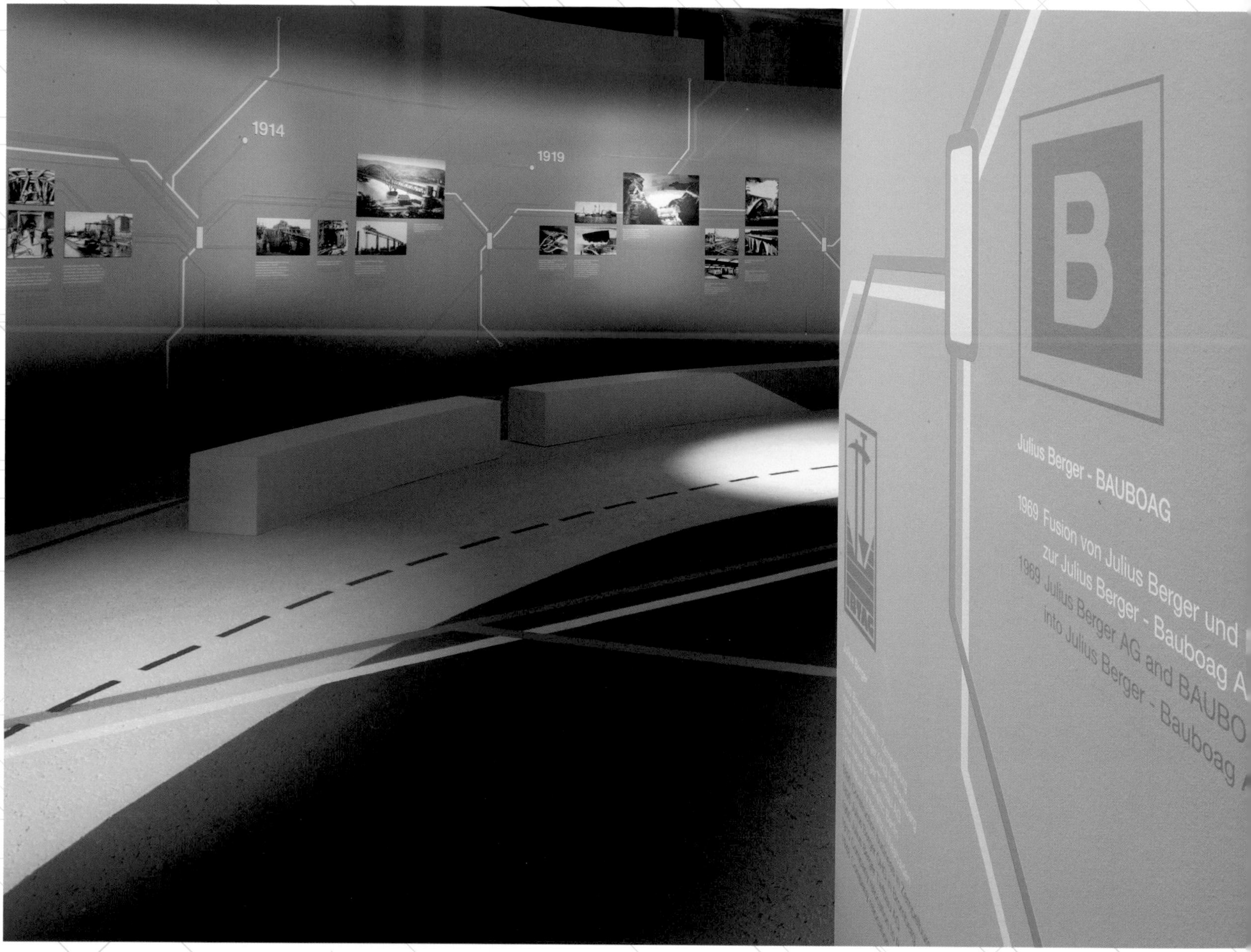

Ingenieurbau
Civil

The Blue Line, a 180-m element of curved blue steel, served as a signpost, guiding visitors and communicating vital information about the history of the company.

VOSS + FISCHER
LINDE: 125 YEARS OF NEW IDEAS
MUNICH, GERMANY

Celebrating Change

As Linde celebrated its 125th anniversary in 2004, the company had already experienced a dynamic internal process of change and reorientation, progressing from being a traditional manufacturer of gases for industrial and pharmaceutical use to fulfilling the role of a major international player in the world of technology. The anniversary celebration was to reflect the company's development and to present current changes and future ambitions in a visible way. Commissioned to realize this event, Frankfurt-based agency Voss + Fischer invited all guests to make a 'Journey through the World of Ideas'. Starting point for the journey was the Linde Gas Division in Höllriegelskreuth, in the southern part of Munich, where in 1879 Carl von Linde had laid the foundation for his subsequent success story. Expressing his personal views on the planning and realization of the event, Claus Fischer of Voss + Fischer recalls that his firm set out to 'design and present the anniversary celebration as an important and strategic cornerstone which would reflect the new positioning of Linde and create a corporate image'.
From the outset, everyone involved agreed that the event should transcend rationality and engage guests in a happening that would touch on all aspects of the company – values, heritage, skills, competence and quality – in an emotional way as well. The aim was an exciting experience full of surprising and inspiring ideas. 'The journey through the world of ideas had to achieve both targets,' says Fischer. 'It had to be simultaneously entertaining and informative. We wanted a solution, therefore, that would convey the spirit of the company and its distinguishing features through a range of unexpected views stretching from past developments to the present situation and on into the future.' More than simply demonstrating abstract goals, the event was designed to present a dynamic process and its impact on the continuing development of Linde.

Below: The Blue Line, running from the entrance through the marquees and ending at a stage, curled it's way through the five Blue Boxes. Bottom: The visual journey through the history of the company was followed by an acoustical experiment.

The celebration started in the car park of the Linde Gas Division, where huge white marquees welcomed the approximately 700 guests. Inside, the so-called 'Blue Line', a 180 m element of curved steel painted in Linde's corporate colours, wound – partly floating, partly fixed – through the 'World of Linde'. Running from the entrance through the marquees and ending at a stage, the line served as a signpost, guiding visitors and communicating vital information about the history of the company.

Balancing the rational approach represented by the Blue Line and the facts it conveyed was an emotional appeal achieved by five Blue Boxes, whose themes were 'the people of Linde' and four business segments: 'Medical Gases/Healthcare', 'Gases', 'Industrial Trucks' and 'Engineering'. Each box featured accessible forms of visualization related to the topic in question. Distinctive symbols were used to make visitors feel and understand the multitude of activities, ideas and achievements attributed to Linde. Symbolizing the people of Linde, for example, was a chair, which suggested the simplicity of ingenious ideas. A forest area was created to symbolize healthcare. Drops of water fell from the ceiling, causing ripples, in a portrayal designed to show Linde's position as the world leader in hydrogen technology. Additional acoustic, olfactory and haptic devices engaged all senses, turning the Blue Boxes into a three-dimensional event zone. The purpose was clear. 'Together, the Blue Line and the Blue Boxes enabled the audience to learn about the history of Linde, as well as about current skills, developments and capabilities,' affirms Fischer. Part of the 'Journey through the World of Ideas' was, of course, the anniversary ceremony itself, which took place in a hall that was predominantly white. White was selected for its symbolic association with innocence, new beginnings and a future waiting to be shaped and filled with ideas and visions. The hall served as a backdrop for keynote speeches, followed by a concerto for cello, chorus and 32 variously pitched Linde gas cylinders. 'A surprising and truly unique idea – turning gas cylinders into musical instruments,' muses Fischer. After the performance, guests moved to a covered terrace for drinks, while seating in the hall was rearranged for the evening's banquet. Leaving no stone unturned, Fischer paid close attention to detail, even in matters of cuisine, such as finger food 'designed' to harmonize with all aspects of the meal and the setting. 'We tried to make the food correspond to the general character of the surroundings and the whole event. The Linde anniversary celebration is proof that planning and realizing a successful event is about more than just arranging a party. An event is always based on a comprehensive strategy, intensive talks, a thoroughly developed concept and communication with the client.' Fischer's explanation is an excellent summary of the way his agency prepares and develops individual solutions for clients who are planning conventions, conferences and other business events.

'A surprising and truly unique idea – turning gas cylinders into musical instruments.'
Claus Fischer

Idea / concept: Voss + Fischer – www.voss-fischer.de
Photographer: Wonge Bergmann

Client: Linde – www.linde.de
Lighting consultant: Neumann & Müller Veranstaltungstechnik
Graphic consultant: desres design group
Multimedia consultant: S.P.O.T. Medien
Capacity: 1000 guests
Total floor area (m²): 2500
Duration of construction: 4 weeks
Start of event: 24 June 2004

This page and opposite: Themes such as the people of Linde and the 4 business segments were symbolized by the simplicity of such things as a drop of water, a chair and a forest.

SUNDHEIT HEALTH

WISSEN KNOWLEDGE WISS
tomorrow

A forest area was created to symbolize healthcare.

Below: The end of the Blue Line marked the end of the 'Journey through the World of Ideas' and the beginning of a ceremony that took place in a predominantly white hall.
Middle and bottom: details from the Blue Boxes.

For a promotional campaign that was to be launched in a gallery in New York's SoHo, Sharp Electronics asked Tronic Studio for an art installation that would not be 'salesy'.

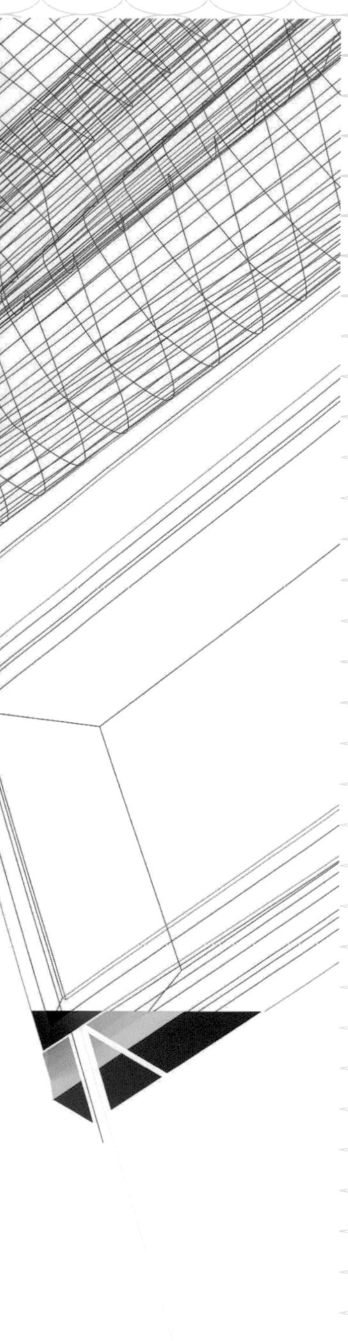

TRONIC STUDIO
BLOOM
NEW YORK CITY, NEW YORK, USA

Everything's Blooming

The Sharp campaign to promote AQUOS Liquid Crystal Television, a project headed by Wieden & Kennedy, featured art installations that incorporated the Japanese manufacturer's LC TVs. Wieden & Kennedy called on branding agency Formavision, which invited New York-based Tronic Studio to get in on the action. 'The brief we got was pretty open,' recalls Jesse Seppi, co-founder of Tronic Studio. 'The client wanted us to use our own language and didn't expect anything "salesy". The only thing Sharp requested was that we find a way to integrate their screens into an art installation.' Accustomed to doing broadcast, film and installation design – sometimes individually, sometimes in interdisciplinary projects – Seppi and partner Vivian Rosenthal were thrilled to be given what virtually amounted to carte blanche. In a gallery space in SoHo, leased especially for the occasion, the team created a multimedia exhibition that explored the parallels between natural phenomena and man-made design. Inspired by the lifelike images produced by AQUOS, Seppi and Rosenthal christened the art installation Bloom and began by researching the late-19th-century Art Nouveau movement. 'The writhing plant forms of Art Nouveau integrate natural shapes with innovations in design,' says Rosenthal. 'Throughout the Art Nouveau movement, there was a tension implicit between the decorative and the modern. You can feel that tension in the work of both designers and architects of that time.' In addition to referencing a relevant historical style, Seppi and Rosenthal wanted to incorporate a reaction to the role that technology plays in our lives today. 'After many years in which human beings saw technological innovations as a way to dominate nature, a shift in our approach arose,' says Seppi, explaining that a current understanding of 'the fragility of our planet' is leading to a more eco-friendly merging of technology and environment.

This page: Tronic Studio translated writhing Art Nouveau-based plant forms into a futuristic polystyrene installation.

To maintain their focus on the essence of the concept, the designers relied on a familiar device: a project-related mantra. The phrase for Bloom was: 'All things synthetic mimic all things organic.' The team set the desired mood by creating a style frame and sourcing reference imagery pertaining to the concept. The example they offer to illustrate this phase of their work is that of a carburettor as a metaphor for the human heart. After finding many such parallels in architecture, product design, the medical field and, says Seppi, 'in the Sharp AQUOS technology itself', they felt sufficiently immersed in the concept to take it to the next level. The animation, which took roughly a month to complete, started with snakelike wires that meandered elegantly towards a large computer-generated mass. As the wires started connecting to the larger structure, an explosion of red – like drops of ink or blood dispersing in water – took over the screen. The crimson 'bloom' clarified the title of the installation.

'Just as the video looped to tell a story of how the bloom was formed,' says Rosenthal, 'the experience of the show itself looped the concept over and over, at both a micro and a macro scale. Video and sculpture worked in tandem – the video being of the digital world and the sculpture demonstrating how the digital turns physical.' Because an actual 'bloom' would have been too costly, if not technically impossible, to recreate as a static 3D sculpture, Tronic Studio selected a more streamlined element from the video. The sculpture depicted the coming together of two flows, one blood-red and organic, the other silver and synthetic. With the aid of 3D Studio MAX software and CNC milling, the animation was brought to life in polystyrene foam. After smoothing the surface of each machine-cut foam component, the designers applied a layer of gel to create a hard shell and added a final coat of automotive paint to obtain an exterior that a grinning Seppi describes as being 'as slick as a Ferrari'.

The goal of the finished piece, says Rosenthal, was to have the viewers' attention go back and forth between the HD video projected on the 127-cm AQUOS screens and the physical sculpture housing them. The Tronic Studio partners fondly recall opening night: 'You could see how people were really absorbing the space with all their senses.' Pleased with the result, the people at Sharp did nothing to conceal their excitement and satisfaction. 'It wasn't anything they could have come up with themselves. But when the project was completed, they really got it.'

'Tronic Studio gets asked to do some extremely cool work,' says Rosenthal, 'but this site-specific installation was definitely one of those projects that gave us a chance to create a total work of art and to combine all our skills in one piece.'

'You could see how people were really absorbing the space with all their senses.'
Tronic Studio

Designer: Tronic Studio – www.tronicstudio.com
Photographer: Peter Field Peck – www.pfpeck.com

Client: Sharp Electronics – www.sharp.com
Curator: Formavision – www.formavision.info
Manufacturer: Kreysler & Associates
Duration of construction: 3 weeks
Start of event: January 2005

A video shown on several 127-cm LCD screens created a context for the sculptural element that highlighted the event, and vice versa.

This page and opposite: viewer's attention was drawn back and forth, up and down, from one part of the installation to another.

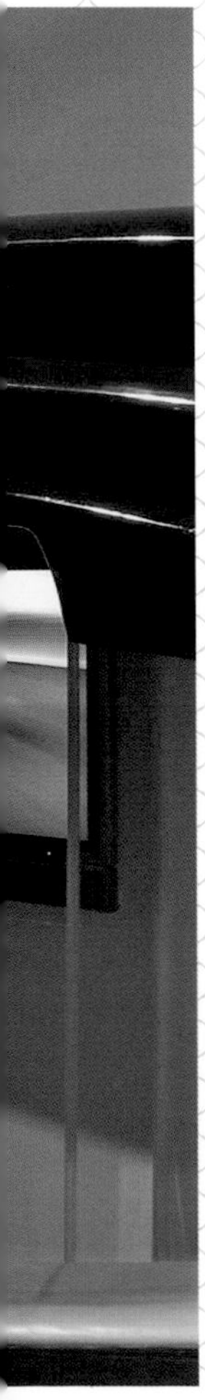

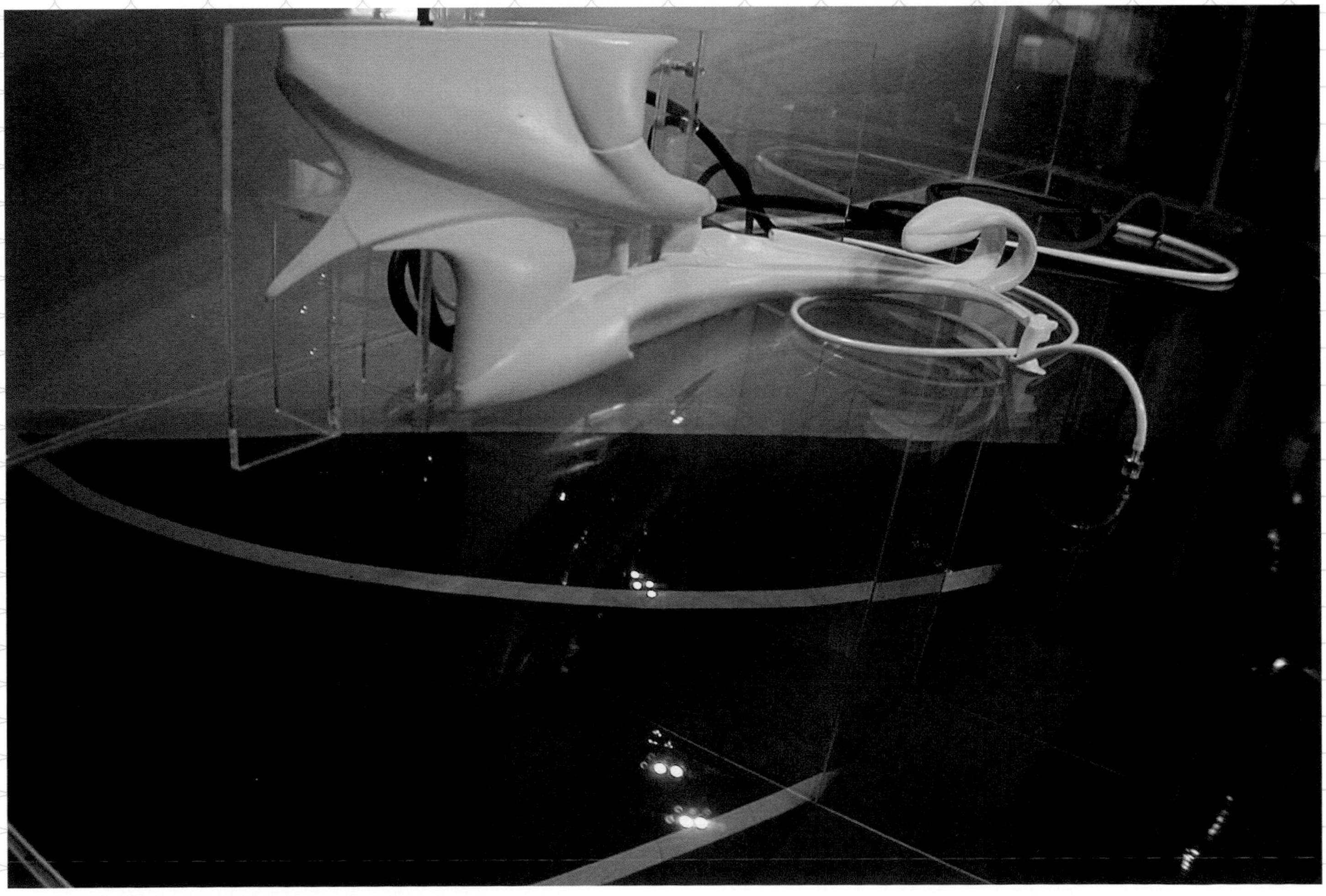

This page: The shape of the golden membrane corresponded to that of Samsung's oval logo, which is usually blue.

SCHMIDHUBER + KAINDL
OLYMPIC RENDEZVOUS @ SAMSUNG
TURIN, ITALY

Go for Gold

The Korean firm of Samsung Electronics is in the premiere league of global players in its sector and, since 1997, has been a 'worldwide partner' of the Olympic Games in the field of wireless communication equipment. The sponsorship, which has covered several editions of the Olympic Games, provides both financial and material support to these international events. In exchange, the Italian National Olympic Committee made available the picturesque Piazza Solferino, a square in the centre of Turin, for the sponsors to establish a base for two weeks during the Winter Games of 2006. Samsung's pavilion, which is specially designed for each venue, has an obvious name: Olympic Rendezvous @ Samsung or OR@S. After four Games in a row, the site became a permanent address, well established among the Olympic community and users of the worldwide web.

The Munich-based company Schmidhuber + Kaindl designed and realized the OR@S pavilion for the Summer Games of 2004, held in Athens. Both in Athens and Turin, the designers made formal use of the company's oval logo and interpreted it spatially. For the Summer Games, a golden ribbon spiralled upwards around huge columns, creating a spectacular outdoor area for public viewing and a daily programme of events. A rectangular white cube behind the golden 'Loop' accommodated the Spectator Centre and the Athlete Centre. In wintry Turin, a heated oval pipe radiated its golden message atop a white base.

The Samsung pavilion fulfils two functions. It is a meeting place where accredited athletes and their associates are received by the sponsor. A place to relax and to watch Olympic events on huge plasma screens in comfort. And it is a showroom for displaying the sponsor's latest products. Both functions require easy access and focus on the 'game' of seeing and being seen.

This page: The latest mobile phones could be tested in the Spectator Centre, a facility located at ground level.

In Italy, this game was played mainly in the Athlete Centre on the upper floor, which featured a gallery and permitted people to look down on the comings and goings in the Spectator Centre below. Guests downstairs could gaze up and catch a glimpse of the gallery and the vaulted ceiling. Two huge oval windows – transparent membranes, tautly stretched – virtually brought the famous façades of Turin, a city known the world over for its architecture, into the pavilion.

With a simple but strong idea – the interpretation of Samsung's two-dimensional logo into an architectural form – backed by excellent references, Schmidhuber + Kaindl had already made its mark with a successful design pitch for Athens. The German company later learned that the initial decision had been influenced not only by its work for Audi and mobile-phone company O_2, but also by the reputation of German design. The team met the client's expectations by playing it safe; they collaborated with longstanding contractual partners and associates in realizing the design. The end result is a new standard in the design and interior architecture of sponsor-related pavilions. The success of the pavilion in Athens prompted Samsung to commission the team to design the venue in Turin, where the formal concept was modified to suit both weather and site without relinquishing the white and gold colour scheme or the spatial interpretation of the logo. This prominent design, which was an undeniable highlight of the Sponsor Village, roused the curiosity of visitors, who were plainly eager to enter the Samsung accommodation. The pavilion attracted over 400,000 visitors in two weeks.

Brand-new mobile phones were on show at the Spectator Centre. The display design was inspired by a wintry landscape and glacial forms. Thanks in part to this apt presentation of cutting-edge products, no Italian mad about his telefonino could have stayed away. Added to that factor was the presence of Alberto Tomba, Italy's most successful downhill skier and Samsung's ambassador to the Winter Games. Fondly known as Tomba la Bomba, the athlete twice won Olympic Gold in the '90s. He staged a rousing show each day at OR@S.

Next stop Beijing. What can we expect from Samsung at the Sponsor Village during the 2008 Olympic Summer Games? And who will make it happen?

The pavilion attracted over 400,000 visitors, partly because no Italian mad about his telefonino wanted to miss seeing the latest Samsung models.

Designer: Schmidhuber + Kaindl – www.schmidhuber.de
Photographer: Gaudenz Danuser – mail@gaudenzdanuser.com

Client: Cheil Communications for Samsung Electronics – www.samsung.com
General contractor: Schmidhuber + Kaindl
Graphic design: Schmidhuber + Kaindl
Audiovisual and media consultant: Winkler Veranstaltungstechnik
Manufacturer: Maedebach Werbungand Nüssli
Operations: Javelin Europe
Floor area (m²): 550 (ground floor), 640 (upper floor)
Duration of construction: 2 months
Start of event: 10 February 2006

Below and opposite bottom: The Athlete Centre, a meeting point for accredited athletes and their families include comfortable lounge chairs and internet stations and a bar.

Below and opposite bottom: The design of the walls and displays was inspired by glaciers and winter landscapes.

Thanks to the Samsung camp's position at the edge of the Piazza Solferino, the striking silhouette of the structure could be seen from afar.

Bro
WiBro Communication
What is WiBro?
Samsung WiBro
Game on your mobile phone
Slim design
hear, see and feel SAMSUNG
imagine making a confident
personal statement with
your phone of fashion

A disco in Ibiza is not what most people envision when they hear the term 'press event'.

DESIGN HOCH DREI
DODGE CALIBER / INT. MEDIA LAUNCH 2006
IBIZA, SPAIN

Driving the Point Home

'Grab life by the horns' is the apt advertising slogan of Dodge, a carmaker whose logo is a ram's head. Previously limited to the American market, Dodge models were rarely seen in other parts of the world. The situation changed in April 2006, however, when the Dodge Caliber was introduced into the international market. Marketing strategists have their sights on Europe. The all-new Dodge Caliber is the car to stage this coup. It is the first of four new models to come out within the next few years. The car is placed in the mid-segment, where competition in Europe and Asia is especially strong. No wonder the press event was highest priority for DaimlerChrysler. DaimlerChrysler invited groups of international journalists to the Mediterranean island of Ibiza for a series of lavish press events, complete with all the trimmings. Within a three-week period, 600 journalists in groups of 40 were briefed and entertained. Right after the press event around 2,200 dealers and sales people were trained at the same set.

The event was organized in-house by parent company DaimlerChrysler and given an 'overall image' by design hoch drei of Stuttgart, a communication-design outfit that has worked with DaimlerChrysler since 1993. 'We have designed many trade-fair stands for them, as well as events for other DaimlerChrysler brands,' says Susanne Wacker of design hoch drei.

The site for the event was rather unusual. Ibiza, a world-famous clubbing capital, was selected for its appeal to the reporters. Activities started with a press conference in the island's legendary Club Pacha, a disco founded in 1973. The conference was followed by a meal and a night at the Pacha Hotel. The next day, journalists were invited to test drive the Caliber and relax at the Dodge House, a Mediterranean villa with pool, massage facilities and Carrera racing.

Setting the mood for the Dodge Caliber sales launch was the corridor leading into the club, where guests were surrounded by blood-red walls paired with a hip font composed of white dots.

'Dodge has a powerful image,' says Wacker. 'The roots of the extreme expressive Dodge brand and the powerful emotionality of the new models gave us the crucial impulse for the design.' Calling the event Heartbeat, a reference to both emotion and power, she and the team went on to develop the bold graphics of their plan.

The colour scheme for the event combined a lush bright red, the key colour at Dodge, with white. Taking centre stage were the words 'Dodge Caliber' in LED type-lettering. Besides graphics and a space for the press conference, the Stuttgart team designed signage for the test-drive track, platforms for show cars, a huge banner for the front of the hotel, and the reception area inside. Their contribution to Dodge House was the planning of all furnishing and the design of the car relay station. They were also responsible for the design of print material: a road book, press folders and a number of other handy items. For the sake of a uniform image, all text appeared in red for this occasion, rather than in the more conventional black.

At the entrance to the disco, a brightly lit Dodge banner greeted guests. A sky of shiny plexiglas banners gave the guests a first hint of what they were about to encounter: something 'anything but cute'. A passageway with a high red partition at one side curved around a bend, leaded guests to their first view of the Dodge Caliber. Poised on a platform, with a light show on the wall behind it, the car was resplendent. A top act. No doubt about it.

Design hoch drei illuminated the 260-m^{2}space with a backdrop of LEDs. 'The LEDs pulsated in time to the music which we had developed together with an acclaimed DJ, and illustrated the heartbeat theme beautifully,' says Wacker. The dotted grid of lights corresponded perfectly to the rest of the graphics, as well as to a number of purposed-designed objects and light design, like a hip retro lamp whose shades consisted of suspended plastic discs. 'The rest of the furnishings were already there and could not be altered,' says Wacker, 'although we did have round, red cushions made for the seating area.'

In addition to gearing the design to the existing space, the team had to create a setting that could be dismantled quickly. They had to take it down once a day, before midnight, to allow Pacha to entertain the regular disco crowd. The back wall was modular but still complicated, because of the LEDs. After the activity-packed day, many of the journalists were probably asleep by midnight, however, dreaming about raunchy, cool Dodge Calibers jumping fences in Ibiza.

'A sky of shiny plexiglas banners gave the guests a first hint of what they were about to encounter: something 'anything but cute' Susanne Wacker

Design: design hoch drei – www.design-hoch-drei.de
Photography: Harry Steininger – www.challenge.de.com

Client: DaimlerChrysler – www.daimlerchrysler.com
Lighting consultants: Light & Magic and Showtec
Graphic consultant: design hoch drei
Media consultant: Light & Magic
Manufacturers: Stadelmayer Werbung and AGMA Messe- und Ausstellungsbau
Total floor area (m^2): 260
Start of event: 17 April 2006

The hotel, in which the journalists stayed, was immersed in red light for the occasion.
A huge banner and conspicuously positioned Dodge Calibers completed the party outfit.

This page and opposite: Total design solution: in addition to planning and implementing an overall image for the launch, design hoch drei was responsible for the signage and for an exhibition at Dodge House.

TONIGHT!
LIVE AT THE PACHA
DANCE CLUB
PACHA

PIT
STOP

This page: From a distance, the curving wall resembled the skateboarders' half-pipe, an image associated with acceleration and freedom of movement.

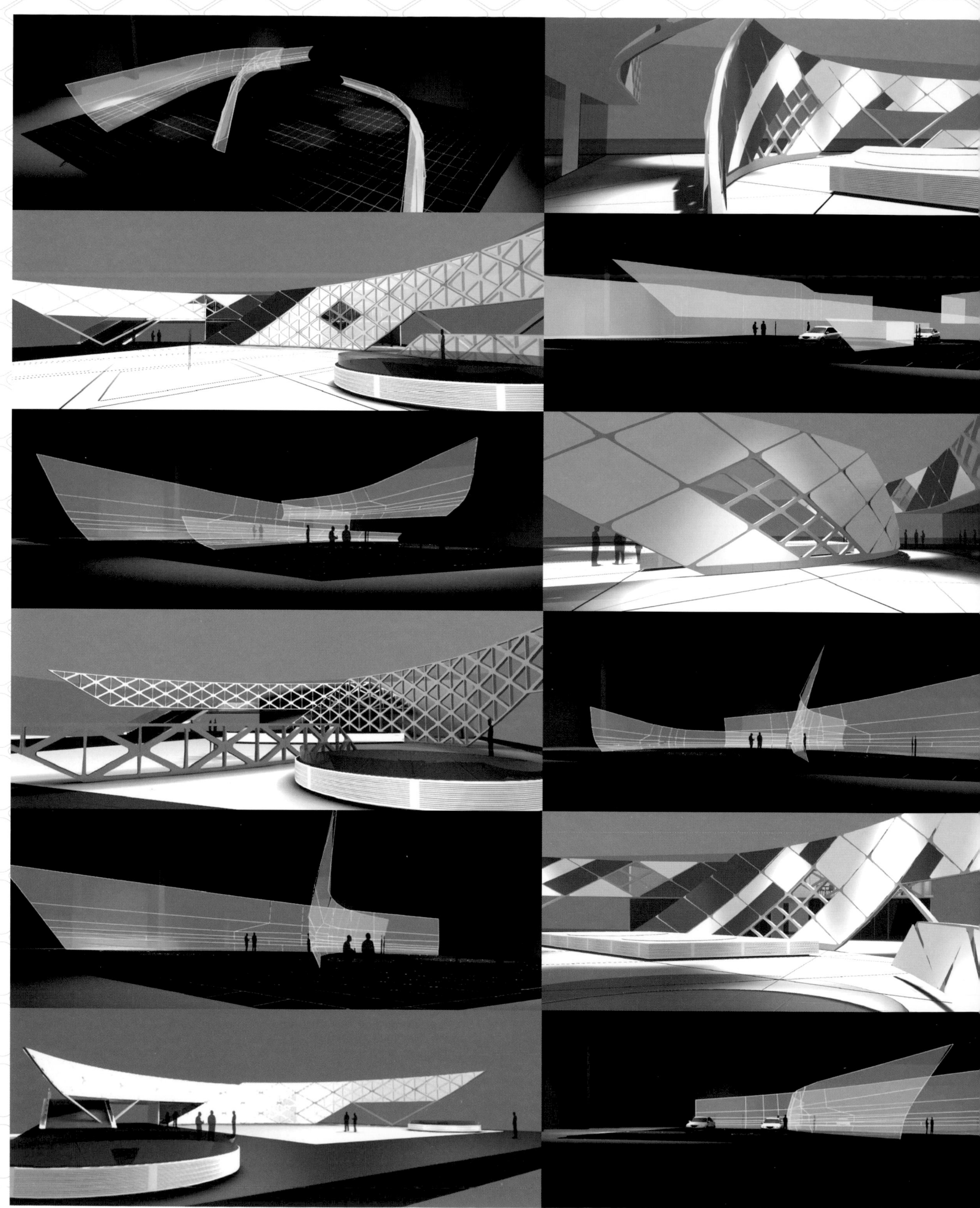

IMAGINATION
THE MAZDA GLOBAL AUTO SHOW
TOKYO, JAPAN

Standing Movement

A car endowed with a psyche would surely become depressed if it were forced to remain still. Immobility is contrary to the essence of a machine created for movement. Despite the protestations of numerous fans and owners, cars do not have psyches. They couldn't care less about moving or standing still. Car manufacturers and car dealers, on the other hand, express an entirely different view. 'A car is more than mere glass, rubber and metal; it must engender dreams and fantasies,' said the new boss of Daimler Chrysler, Dieter Zetsche, in a recent interview. And it follows that a car does that best as it speeds along the motorway or around a race track. When an automobile is stationary, as at a trade fair, it is infinitely more difficult to propel the observer's imagination beyond glass, rubber and metal. Even the best-designed vehicle has its limitations, although today's car makers are constantly giving their latest models fresh momentum in the form of dynamic lines, sleek silhouettes and interiors tailored to match.

Because cars at trade fairs and in showrooms move only on turntables, at best, the logical task of the stand or showroom designer is to create an environment that 'moves' the visitor. Successful but highly cost-intensive efforts have been made in this direction. The results are visible at all major automotive events, whether in Frankfurt, Geneva, Detroit or Tokyo. Dynamism, movement and energy are no longer latent attributes relating only to the cars on display; they apply equally to the relevant trade-fair stands and showrooms.

Such considerations led Japanese car manufacturer Mazda to the design of a stand that expresses Zoom-Zoom, an alliterative term coined to convey brand identity. Intended to reawaken childhood memories of the 'emotion of motion', the word 'zoom' – as in 'zoom in' and 'zoom out' – also implies the possibility of movement within stillness. As objects approach or recede, the focus of an event changes without the need for the onlooker to move.

Unlike the conventional linear display that dominates many trade-fair stands, the diamond grid caught the eye by presenting vehicles at dynamic angles.

Mazda saw the concept as an interesting basis for displaying the firm's latest models, including the MX5 roadster and the RX8, with its rotary-piston engine.

The dominant architectural element of the trade-fair stand that Mazda introduced at the Tokyo Motor Show of October 2005 – an event at which the company focused special attention on the Senku sports car – was the so-called Motion Wall. This panoramic backdrop swept visitors into a 'primal experience' marked by movement. When viewed from a distance, the curving, 35-m-long wall resembled the skateboarders' half-pipe, an image associated with acceleration and freedom of movement, especially in the minds of the young. Dynamic, elegant and light, the wall was pierced by lozenge-shaped openings that corresponded to the pattern on the floor: extending this diamond-like grid gave the stand an added dimension of spaciousness and had an energizing effect on visitors.

The Motion Wall, which featured built-in LED screens, doubled as a projection surface for the display of brand and product presentations. Aimed at a younger target audience were light shows and vibrant images of dancers, athletes and skateboarders: projected onto the entire wall, they illustrated Mazda's successful transformation into a brand for all ages.

They used sheet metal to create simpler forms, such as revolve surrounds, partitions and furniture. The central floor space, with its diamond-like grid, was finished in white and silver laminate. A reference to the design of the previous scheme was the use of black-bamboo panels, whose dimensions matched those of traditional Japanese tatami. Unlike the pattern dominating the central area, these panels took the shape of an orthogonal grid and, thanks to their origins and texture, provided a contrast to the predominantly man-made materials found elsewhere at the stand.

Behind the design and realization of the Mazda Global Car Show is the renowned international communication and brand agency Imagination, which is also responsible for the trade-fair stands of other Ford Group brands: Ford, Land Rover, Jaguar, Aston Martin, Lincoln (USA) and Mercury (USA). Imagination's Group Creative Director, Douglas Broadley said about the project: 'This was an exciting project to work on, especially as Mazda is such a innovative and insightful brand. Our inspiration for the stand was taken from contemporary Japanese design - with simplistic, clean lines being used complimented by a vibrant colour palette and modern materials. Key pieces of multimedia were built into the architectural environment to emphasise a sense of movement and bring the whole "Zoom Zoom" brand essence to life!'

Following its premiere at the Tokyo Motor Show and its appearance at the Detroit Motor Show, the largest event of its kind in the world, Mazda's Zoom-Zoom stand will welcome visitors to all international automotive trade fairs for some time to come.

'As an example of temporary architecture that was integrated with specially created content, this was one of the most exciting projects to work on.' Miles Dutton - Creative Lead

Designer: Imagination – www.imagination.com
Photographer: Mark Livemore for Imagination – www.imagination.com

Client: Mazda – www.mazda.com
Key creative team: Douglas Broadley, Miles Dutton (Creative Lead), Simon Woods, Philip Sinclair, Eiko Fujita Summers, Brian Griver, Kenny McAndrew, Paul Gowers, Morag Crichton, Andrew McKinna, Tanya Burns, John Pickering, Peter Brooks, Clare Johnston and Paul Quain
Engineer: Posselt Consult
Total floor area (m^2): 1794
Duration of construction: 9 days
Start of event: 19 October 2005

Lozenge-shaped patterns contributed to the dynamism of the trade-fair stand.

Advanced Driver-Support
Technologies
Digest

This page: The central architectural element of Mazda's Zoom-Zoom stand was the Motion Wall.

This page: Mission accomplished: a unified presentation highlighted a diversity of products.

This page and opposite: Jonas Pinzke, creative director of Swedish agency Knock, warns us to avoid being lagom, or 'mainstream'.

The Volvo C30 is a car whose preliminary design was first outlined at the Detroit Motor Show. It will go into production and be marketed at the end of 2006. The sporty two-door is a smaller Volvo that should appeal to a much younger market than is usual for Volvo. In the past, Volvo dealers have had little contact with this younger target group. Activities surrounding the Volvo C30 were intended to draw the dealers' attention to these new clients. The main event was structured to mirror the participants' uncertainty and their keen air of expectation, as well as to deliberately highlight a world in flux: a market that is hovering between chaos and a sense of wellbeing. 'The event has been designed as the line of a heartbeat,' says Pinzke. 'In order to get the target group out of its comfort zone, we stretched every detail to the max and worked with contrasts.'

The Volvo C30 Experience was held in an old boat shed in Gothenburg harbour. All participants were ferried to the venue by boat. The building, enveloped in white fabric, revealed no sign of Volvo or the event itself. Guests were led into the building through a tunnel lined with white fabric and soft grey carpeting. A purpose-created, mellifluous sound installation spread a sense of wellbeing. Given a welcome that matched the motto 'everything except "lagom", visitors entering the building encountered a programme of contrasts: another dark container tunnel, 50 m long, with LED strips as the only lighting, and a hard floor. Here the soundscape provided another contrast, as weird dissonances reverberated from bare metal walls. Having reached the 9-x-52-m main hall, dealers found the longer walls lined in 54 used, somewhat rusty, 6-m-long transport containers: each side had nine rows composed of colourfully jumbled containers stacked three high. The two shorter sides served as 9-x-5-m projection screens. A 150-m-long white conveyor belt meandering through the room carried culinary delicacies, which alternated with objects of particular interest to the young target group. On either side of this moving ribbon of goodies were groups of elegant, white-leather lounge furniture: 154 pieces in all.

After they had entered the space, taken their seats and been greeted by a short speech, guests were shown a 90-minute film about the world of the Volvo C30. Every now and then, the film was interrupted by one of six two-minute films, which abruptly cut into the otherwise calm flow of the presentation. Here, too, was a play on opposites: tranquillity and restlessness. As their arrival at the building suggested, the participants, tensely expectant, never got to see the car itself – not at any point during the evening. Not a product photograph. Not even a Volvo logo.

'We wanted the audience to picture the car in their mind,' says Pinzke. 'The product, along with product images and logos, was banned. However, all bits and pieces that we presented did reflect the car in some way or another.'

'All bits and pieces that we presented did reflect the car in some way or another.' Jonas Pinzke

Designer: Knock – www.knock.se
Photographer: Mikael Olsson – www.mikaelolsson.se

Client: Volvo Cars – www.volvocars.com
Consultants: Primetec and Ashton
Engineer: Space Display
Manufacturer: Space Display
Facilities: Lounge
Capacity: 220 guests
Total floor area (m²): 468
Duration of construction: 10 days
Start of event: 19 April 2006

Not a single image of the Volvo C30 was shown at the event.
This picture gives you a glance at the car the experience was all about.

P A2 21 0

Below and opposite top: Welcome to the world of the target group.
Bottom and opposite bottom: A 50-m long, dark container tunnel through which visitors entered the building was in contrast with the main hall.

Black cars awash in green light made for a simple yet highly effective scheme.

KMS
MYTHS: AUTOMOBILI LAMBORGHINI
MUNICH, GERMANY

Illusions From Italy

In June 2004, a black crack as wide as a door appeared on a white wall in the Neue Sammlung, the design wing of Munich's Pinakothek der Moderne. The dimly lit shaft behind it descended to an eerily dark space in the basement. Only when their eyes began to adjust to the darkness were visitors able to make out the greenish outlines of a sports car in the middle of the room.
Here, in the so-called Schaudepot – an underground area of the museum normally accessed only by those authorized to view the more esoteric items in the collection – was an exhibition entitled Myths: Automobili Lamborghini. More like an installation than a conventional exhibition, the show featured only seven of Lamborghini's legendary racing cars, and these seven were reduced to cleverly illuminated silhouettes.
The creators of the spatial installation was KMS, a Munich-based design studio. 'We had already done the corporate design for the Pinakothek and had been working for Lamborghini since 1998,' say's KMS's creative director Michael Keller. 'When the people at Neue Sammlung came up with the idea for this exhibition, they naturally approached us.'
The seven Lamborghini models, which were selected in consultation with the exhibition designers, illustrated the various stages in the development of these cars since the 1960s. Enthroned on a base made of 8-cm-high nails at the centre of the square space was the latest model, the Murciélago. Lining the sides of the room were six black cars, each poised on a black L-shaped dais and shielded from the centre of the space by a 1.80-m-high wall punctured with a vertical slit: a kind of peephole.

Black magic: the Lamborghini Murciélago balances on a bed of nails.

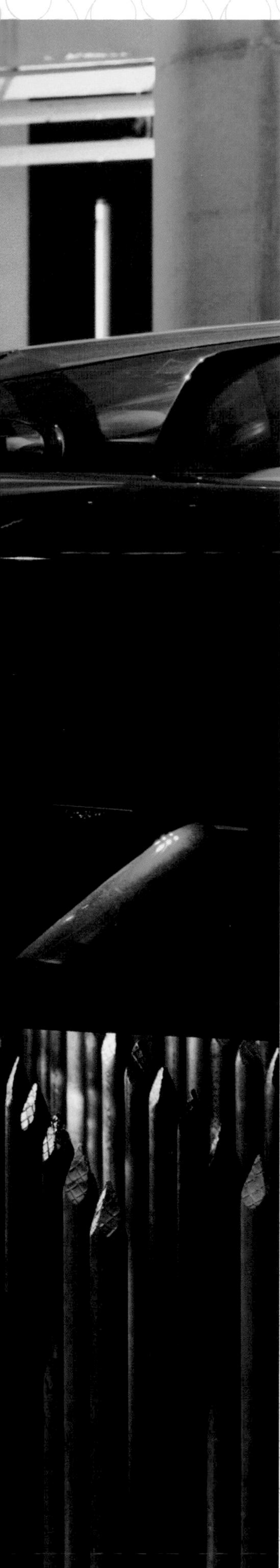

Thus the six cars on the periphery were only vaguely visible from the centre of the room. Visitors who wanted to see them properly had to move in closer, both to view the vehicles and to read the explanatory texts on the walls behind them. Darkness engulfed the entire installation except for the pool of green light surrounding each car and accentuating its contours. The autos could not be seen clearly, for that was not the goal of the installation. It marked the start of a series of Pinakothek exhibitions devoted to myth. 'Our intention was not a car show as such,' says Keller. 'We wanted to feature the growing cult status of this brand.' The muted-green backdrop wrapped the world's fascination with Lamborghinis in a comprehensive spatial experience that encompassed the flamboyance of fast racing cars, the roar of the twelve-cylinder engine, the relatively few models seen on the street, and the strange history of the firm, which is a myth in itself. Following World War II, Ferruccio Lamborghini began his career by making refrigerators and tractors out of scrap metal. His first sports car appeared in the early '60s, to the amusement of rival Ferrari. It was only when the Miura came out in 1966 that the foundation stone was laid for the legend.

The Miura took pride of place in the installation. Whereas the other six cars had lighting that did not vary, green light travelled over the Miura like a giant scanner, sizing up its streamlined form. The brand-new Murciélago, poised on its bed of nails, was another highlight. 'We wanted to project an image of inaccessibility,' explains Keller, adding that the presentation of this car shows a design that has been 'taken to extremes'. A film projected at a height of 4 m – images from the film appeared on the walls above the 'acceleration sculptures' – showed Luc Donckerwolke, Lamborghini's chief designer and the creator of the Murciélago, running over the contours of the individual models. 'But just the contours,' says Keller. 'Rather than showing detailed design drawings, we simply underlined the sketchy nature of the installation. Green light was chosen for the same reason. We wanted to play down the luxury aspect as much as possible. Green was beautifully alienating and emphasized the darkness.'

Finding the cars for the show – seven black Lamborghinis – entailed a long, hard search. 'At first our research focused on the fan clubs. In the end, we borrowed most of the cars from private individuals from all over the world. The Miura came from Canada, the Countach from Italy and the Espada from Belgium.'

As expected, not every visitor appreciated the subfusc presentation of the Lamborghini collection. 'Many people came to look at the cars. And the hall could never have been bright enough for the real sports-car fanatics,' says Keller wryly. 'So we were bombarded with complaints from visitors who wanted more direct information and cars fully visible, down to the smallest detail. What we did was to stage the myth, the mysterious nature and beauty of Lamborghini cars.'

'We staged the myth, the mysterious nature and beauty of Lamborghini cars.' Michael Keller

Designer: KMS – www.kms-team.de
Photographers: Ulrike Myrzik & Manfred Jarisch – www.myrzikundjarisch.com
Jens Bruchhaus

Client: Die Neue Sammlung – www.die-neue-sammlung.de,
Staatliches Museum für angewandte Kunst
Lighting consultant: Limelight
Engineer: KMS
Manufacturer: A&A Expo International
Total floor area (m²): 560
Duration of construction: 4 days
Start of event: 24 June 2004

This page and opposite: Drawing the line: adorning the walls were filmed images that showed chief designer Luc Donckerwolke sketching the contours of the cars.

Klappen
Bezug
integriert konkrete
öffnenden Flügeltüren oder
auch grundsätzliche Charakterzüge,
und die Proportionen des Diablo werden mit
fließenden Konturen des Miura
So entsteht erstmals ein Modell, das so etwas wie den Gencode
trägt; und auch der ursprüngliche Gedanke
zu bauen, deren extreme Leistung ein
Attribut ist wie ihre kompromisslose, puristische

This page and opposite: Not an exhibition but the celebration of a myth, the event featured green light, which accentuated the aura of the Lamborghini models on display.

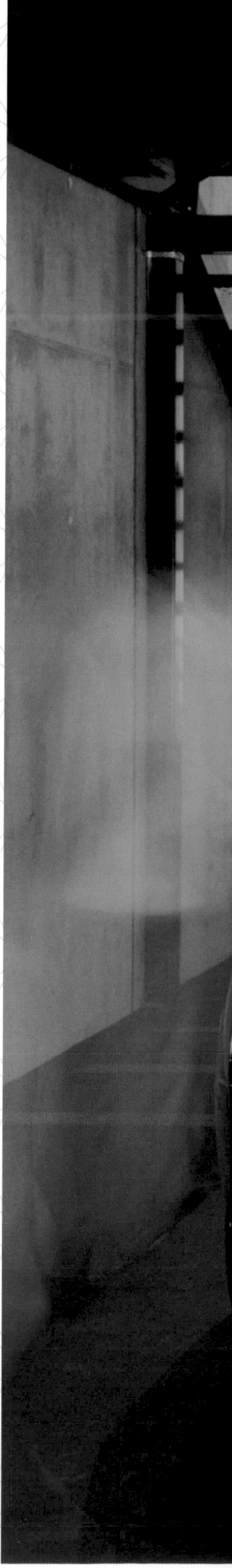

Lamborghini

The act of creating physical spaces was an integral component of Project Fox.

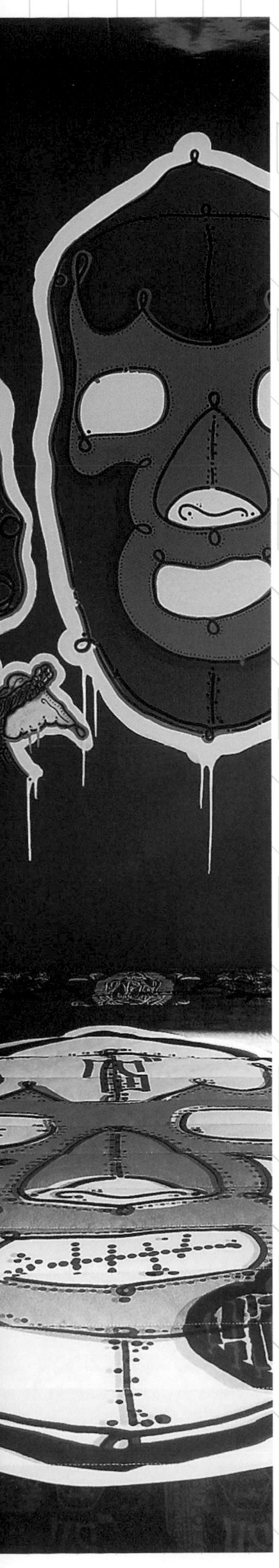

EVENTLABS
PROJECT FOX
COPENHAGEN, DENMARK

Young creatives in Action

In 2005, Volkswagen Group asked forward-thinking German marketing company eventlabs to design and realize what must have seemed like a dream project: the launch of the VW Fox in Europe. Already highly successful in Brazil, the Fox, designed especially for in-town and other short-distance driving, needed to grab the attention of young people in the market for their first car. Instead of presenting the car to the international press at a luxurious but predictable event in a first-class hotel, eventlabs suggested to distribute the budget for the campaign among members of the young target group by inviting students, chefs, urban artists, fashion designers, architects and musicians to Copenhagen, Denmark, to create a unique lifestyle destination for twenty-somethings: the Hotel Fox. Hailing from Norway, Germany, France and places as far away as Brazil, Australia and the United States, the hand-picked participants included those. Most of these young creatives, who fit the target-group profile to a T, express themselves through alternative and demographically relevant platforms like street art and digitally generated animated characters.
The owners of the existing, rather drab hotel courageously agreed to a total overhaul in which they had no say whatsoever. After the old contents of the hotel had been given away at an on-site handout to residents of Copenhagen (a press-worthy occasion in itself) and the interior had been all but gutted, the 21 participants had three months in which to turn the hotel into a destination for young travellers that would capture the world's attention. While the working methods varied as greatly as the nationalities of those contributing to the project, electricity was in the air and everyone agreed that magic was materializing. On-site activity and a shared deadline heightened the sense of camaraderie.

This page: From redesigning hotel rooms to customizing the VW Fox – the result being a number of 'art cars' – the focus of this promotional campaign was on making something truly unique.

'Time was a challenge,' admits Fabian Tank, one of the managing directors of eventlabs. How did he manage to keep the participants motivated throughout a stressful project that included little downtime? 'By generating a supportive environment for everyone and by infecting people with the spirit of creating something truly exceptional,' he replies, adding that his team replaced 'rigid project management with counsel, guidance and loyalty'. Key to the success of the Hotel Fox was the similarity between the eventlabs team and the young protagonists refurbishing the interior, as well as the authenticity that both sides brought to their work. The similarity stopped, however, inside hotel rooms whose décors ranged from marvellously minimal (Norway's Kim Hiorthøy effectively limited his scheme to an almost monochromatic white and red) to cartoon-inspired (witty French illustrator Geneviéve Gauckler painted her trademark black silhouettes on the walls of three rooms). With a three-dimensional installation or two thrown in for good measure, the result radiated a strong pop sensibility that permeated each space, regardless of the designer's source of inspiration.

While work went on at the Hotel Fox, a select number of those invited were attending to Studio Fox. For this element of the campaign, seven individuals and/or teams of artists had been given carte blanche to convert seven VW Foxes into art installations. The site was a vacant industrial warehouse. When roughly 740 members of the international press – divided into smaller groups that were hosted separately over a period of three weeks – arrived in Copenhagen for eventlabs VW Fox extravaganza, the warehouse was their home base between test drives. It was here, in the midst of conceptual Fox installations, that the journalists were served lunch, listened to lectures, relaxed and mingled. Each 'art car' had a matching 'art container', which not only played an important role in the overall exhibition but also added to the mobility of the show: cars in containers can be transported easily to the following events, wherever they might be held.

The turnout for this elaborate, ongoing presentation was quite understandably much larger than that of an average automobile-industry launch. The mix of creative disciplines, venues and sheer vibrancy drew as much media attention from the fashion, design and lifestyle sectors as it did from the targeted trade press. At night, the entire crowd flocked to Club Fox, a restaurant supervised by celebrity chef Stefan Marquard that doubled as a popular nightspot where the party raged for three exciting weeks. Tank attributes the success of the club to the very nature of Project Fox, which was 'all about human interaction, interdisciplinary collaboration and authenticity'. The various activities, he adds, 'were based upon strong ties within the local cultural scene'.

The success of Project Fox as a whole, on the other hand, lies in its more-than-temporary character. The Hotel Fox did not close its doors after the main event was over. Visitors to Copenhagen can still book a room in a place originally designed to promote a Volkswagen, and fall asleep without feeling trapped in an advertising campaign.

The 21 creatives had three months in which to turn the hotel into a destination for young travellers that would capture the world's attention.

Design: eventlabs – www.eventlabs.com
Photography: diephotodesigner.de – www.diephotodesigner.de

Client: Volkswagen – www.volkswagen.com, www.project-fox.org
Start of event: 2 April 2005

This page and opposite: Each artist produced a space marked by his or her favourite technique. The end result included projects featuring collage, silhouettes, cartoons, monochromatic art and, in some cases, complete 3D installations

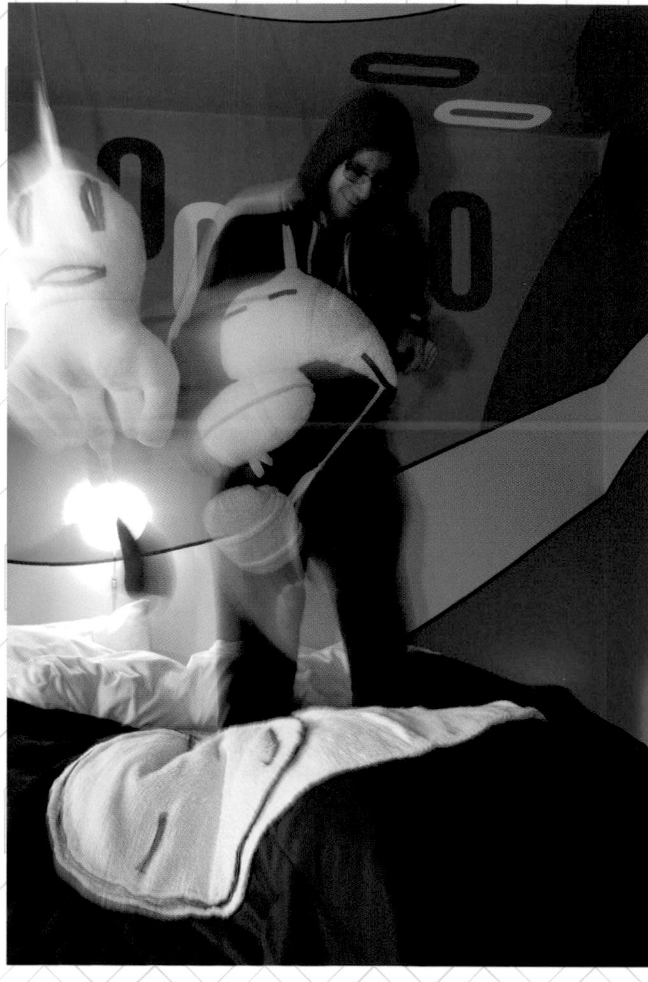

This page and opposite: Club Fox – Vital to the success of the project was the integration of local nightlife into the activities that made up this event.

The overture: a wide expanse enhanced by classical music and a black limousine.

UNIPLAN HONG KONG
LAUNCH OF MERCEDES-BENZ S-CLASS MODEL
WANCHAI, HONG KONG

Leadership. Unlike any other.

'Imagine a place where prosperity and luxury have no boundaries. You are envisaging Hong Kong where its unrivalled blend of technology and finest services creates an extraordinary lifestyle. Savour this premium existence with Mercedes-Benz – a true reflection of discerning taste.' The words come from DaimlerChrysler, makers of a wide range of passenger cars, including the Mercedes S-Class.
In September 2005, Uniplan Hong Kong organized and staged the presentation of the latest model. As an agency that had previously worked with DaimlerChrysler, Uniplan had been invited to tender for the commission. The slogan for the event was 'Leadership. Unlike any other', which referred to both the invited guests and the many technological innovations of the brand since the creation of the S-Class.
The launch was celebrated at the Hong Kong Convention and Exhibition Centre, a venue that Uniplan draped in ceremonial black. Arriving guests walked along 'the innovation path', an arcade that led to the main hall. Images on one side of the asymmetrically arched passage depicted the development of the S-Class and the city of Hong Kong. Lining the other side was a lounge with comfortable seating and intimate candlelight. At the end of the path, visitors caught sight of the entire hall, where a spirited group of musicians played classical music on a dais that fronted a Mercedes-Benz 600 Pullman from the 1960s. Along one side of the room, seven shiny white columns formed a half oval. Opposite them, three gleaming cubes hung from the ceiling. The other longitudinal wall featured an exhibition of large black-and-white photographs from the 1950s, showing people with vintage Mercedes-Benz models. Glasses in hand, served by the friendly waitstaff, guests took their seats or wandered through the dimly lit space, which ultimately held the entire 1200 invitees.

'The innovation path' offered guests an overview of the history of Hong Kong and of the development of Mercedes-Benz models through more than half a century.

With the room filled to capacity, the lights gradually went up, the music swelled and the seven columns rose into the air to reveal seven legendary S-Class models, presented as if they were museum exhibits. After a theatrical pause, the music swelled again, the lighting became even more dramatic and the undersides of the three cubes opened and floated gently to the floor. The three brand-new S-Class models poised on these platforms received a rapturous welcome. Two projection screens and a number of subtle LED pillars added to the striking scene. Among the crowd were the proud owners of the seven vintage cars on show – a select group flown in especially for the event.

The extremely high safety standards that apply to all S-Class models are exemplified by the three-point seat belt, the ABS braking system, airbags, EPS, PRE-SAFE and PRO-SAFE. Similar standards apply to the launch of a new model, and DaimlerChrysler knew it was in safe hands with Uniplan. The event clearly reflected the auto maker's corporate identity and the Mercedes-Benz slogan 'Yesterday's Heritage Is Today's Innovation'. The aim was to generate as many orders as possible for the new S-Class, and the Hong Kong agency appealed directly to up-market clients and their predominantly conservative values. This goal was achieved by conveying the sense of tradition surrounding the luxury brand and by embedding this reference in a formal setting enhanced by classical music.

Uniplan's project manager reports that the brief was short and sweet, that the initial design was realized as planned and that collaboration with DaimlerChrysler went without a hitch. It's a well-known fact that people with similar personalities or common cultural backgrounds tend to get along well. If the same is true of companies, the good relationship between Uniplan and DaimlerChrysler just may be linked to a piece of common history: both German companies opened branches in Hong Kong in 1986. At the time, Hans Brühe was at the helm of Uniplan. The trade-fair specialist had recognized the market potential in Central and Eastern Europe, as well as in Asia, and had set up shop in the main trading centres. In 1986 Hans's son, Christian Brühe (the current CEO and president of Uniplan), was still with Roland Berger, a German group of strategy consultants, but four years later Christian joined his father's firm and went on to expand it. His experience as a consultant to large companies has been crucial in Uniplan's promise to furnish its clients with 'measurable success'. The company's headquarters are in Cologne, Germany, but it has subsidiaries in Stuttgart, Basel, Budapest, Paris, Beijing, Shanghai, Taipei and Hong Kong. At present Uniplan, which has some 500 employees, devotes itself almost exclusively to designing events and trade fairs for companies worldwide. The next step forward would include the continuation of its design of one-off events to further strengthen corporate identity, as well as the type of long-term consultation work that would reinforce the company's image at an even higher level globally.

Among the crowd were the proud owners of the seven vintage cars on show – a select group flown in especially for the event.

Designer: Uniplan Hong Kong – www.uniplan.com.hk
Photographer: H.G. Esch – www.hgesch.de

Client: Mercedes-Benz Hong Kong – www.mercedes-benz.com.hk
Consultant: in-house creative team
Engineer: in-house creative team
Capacity: 1200 guests
Total floor area (m²): 3100
Duration of construction: 45 hours
Start of event: 30 September 2005

Below left: The yellow arches of 'the innovation path' led the guests to the main hall.
Below right: Seven shiny white columns concealed the seven vintage cars.
Bottom: The lounge had comfortable seating and intimate candlelight.

This page: Three brand-new S-Class models on platforms were lowered from the ceiling and revealed to the guests.

In a lead-up to the grand finale, seven columns ascended as the stars below began to shine.

180
1954

The small globe travelled around the world, announcing the 2006 FIFA World Cup, a major sporting event in Germany.

3DELUXE
FOOTBALL GLOBE GERMANY / FOOTBALL GLOBE 2006 FIFA WORLD CUP TOKYO, PARIS, MILAN, ZURICH / FIFA WORLD CUP HOST CITIES, GERMANY

Keep the Ball Rolling

Germany won its bid to host the 2006 FIFA World Cup by a narrow margin: the vote was 12 to 11 in favour of Germany over rival South Africa, with one abstention. To present Germany as a cosmopolitan, good-natured host, the German Football Federation (DFB) commissioned Austrian agency Artevent, headed by André Heller, to stage a closing ceremony celebrating the victory, an event that was held in the summer of 2000. Six months later, the newly formed organizing committee, chaired by football legend Franz Beckenbauer, and the German government launched a programme of football-related art and culture. Selected to curate the programme, Heller culled 48 proposals from the 400 submitted. These four dozen were to be implemented by the DFB Cultural Foundation. One was a project of his own: Football Globe 2006 FIFA World Cup. Heller's accessible installation was to travel through Germany's 12 World Cup cities from 2003 until the first blast of the whistle in Munich in 2006, spreading football fever to the four corners of a nation of poets and philosophers. To achieve this goal, Heller built his concept on generally recognizable and popular images, fusing them into a single symbol that embodied three keywords: sphere = football = globe. Translated into temporary architecture this meant: Telstar = Hexa-Pent. Telstar is the name of the classic football designed for the 1970 World Cup in Mexico, which is composed of twelve black pentagons and 20 white hexagons and still regarded as an icon in football design. The so-called 'truncated icosahedron', generally associated with Buckminster Fuller's experimental architectural work, also brings a holistic world view into play.

The globe, which featured semi-transparent and black-tinted acrylic-resin panels, was held aloft by a curvaceous fiberglass-laminate base.

The geodesic design of the Football Globe was appreciated in an official statement of the Buckminster Fuller Institute. Towards dusk, the football turned into a globe as flexible LED tubes in its air-filled panels lit up in the darkness, displaying the outlines of the world's continents. Artevent commissioned design agency 3deluxe to create the interior of the football, a space literally bursting with media appeal. The dynamic use of forms by the Wiesbaden agency contrasted strongly with the static geometry of the steel construction. A stage positioned at the height of the equator on the Football Globe drew visitors into a black-domed area that seemed to be a combination of planetarium and nightclub. By day, sounds and colours within the space gradually changed in sync with projections on the surrounding walls and the sounds of the ten interactive games that 3deluxe had integrated into the globular pavilion. The theme of Heller's design brought to life the FIFA World Cup motto – 'A time to make friends' – as did evening events inside the football, such as readings, concerts and discussions open to the public for a small entrance fee. In another attempt to reinforce the motto, Franz Beckenbauer and a delegation from the organizing committee visited all 31 qualifying countries to congratulate them and to keep them abreast of the ongoing preparations. Dieter Brell, a co-founder of 3deluxe and the head of 3deluxe interior, picked up Beckenbauer's cosmopolitan signals and suggested to Heller that a further cultural initiative could be developed for the DFB: a smaller globe to be sent abroad on a promotional tour. The idea led to Football Globe Germany, a little brother for Football Globe 2006 FIFA World Cup.

At first glance, the smaller version appeared to replicate the Heller globe, but on closer inspection, it bore all the organically inspired hallmarks of 3deluxe. The globe, which featured semi-transparent and black-tinted acrylic-resin panels, was held aloft by a curvaceous fibreglass-laminate base. A simplified map of the world was printed on the outer surface of the panels, which were adorned with an ornamental white grid highlighted by a floral pattern. Inside, filigreed light strips emitted pulsating bursts of light. In front of one of the three touch screens inserted in the base of the installation was a real corner flag, where visitors could perform a 'corner flag dance' in front of a camera. They were encouraged to email the resulting clip to friends. On 3 October 2005, the day on which Germans celebrate the union of East and West Germany, a temporary lifestyle centre opened in Tokyo as part of the city's German-Japanese Year. German art, design and fashion were on show, targeting a young Japanese audience. This was the first venue of Football Globe Germany, which had a place of honour in the garden. The globe subsequently appeared in front of the Eiffel Tower in Paris, on the Piazza del Duomo in Milan, and in Zürich's main station, proclaiming the coming sport spectacle to all passers-by.

Artevent, 3deluxe and Franz Beckenbauer joined hands, so to speak, to bring to life the FIFA World Cup motto: 'A time to make friends'.

Designer: 3deluxe – www.3deluxe.de
Photographers: Isa Schäfer, Christian Bauer, Frank Robichon, Emanuel Raab and Wolfgang Stahl

Football Globe Germany 2006 FIFA World Cup
Client: Art + Sports / Artevent
Lighting and graphic consultants: 3deluxe interior, 3deluxe graphics
Audiovisual and media consultant: Meso
Engineer: 3deluxe
Manufacturer: Gecco Scene Construction
Duration of construction (including planning): 5 months
Start of event: 3 October 2005

Football Globe 2006 FIFA World Cup
Client: Artevent – www.artevent.at
Lighting consultants: Lightlife and Lightpower
Graphic consultants: 3deluxe graphics and Screenbow
Audiovisual and media consultants: Meso, Fiftyeight 3D, P2, Ekkehard Ehlers and Hagü Schmitz xound
Engineer: Mero
Manufacturers: Mero, Gecco Scene Construction
Capacity: 200 guests standing, 100 guests seated
Total floor area (m²): 140
Duration of construction (including planning): 18 months
Start of event: 13 September 2003

This page and opposite: Inside the big globe, a stage, projected images and ten interactive games made for a fun-filled arena that invited guests to enjoy themselves while warming to the idea of the upcoming FIFA World Cup.

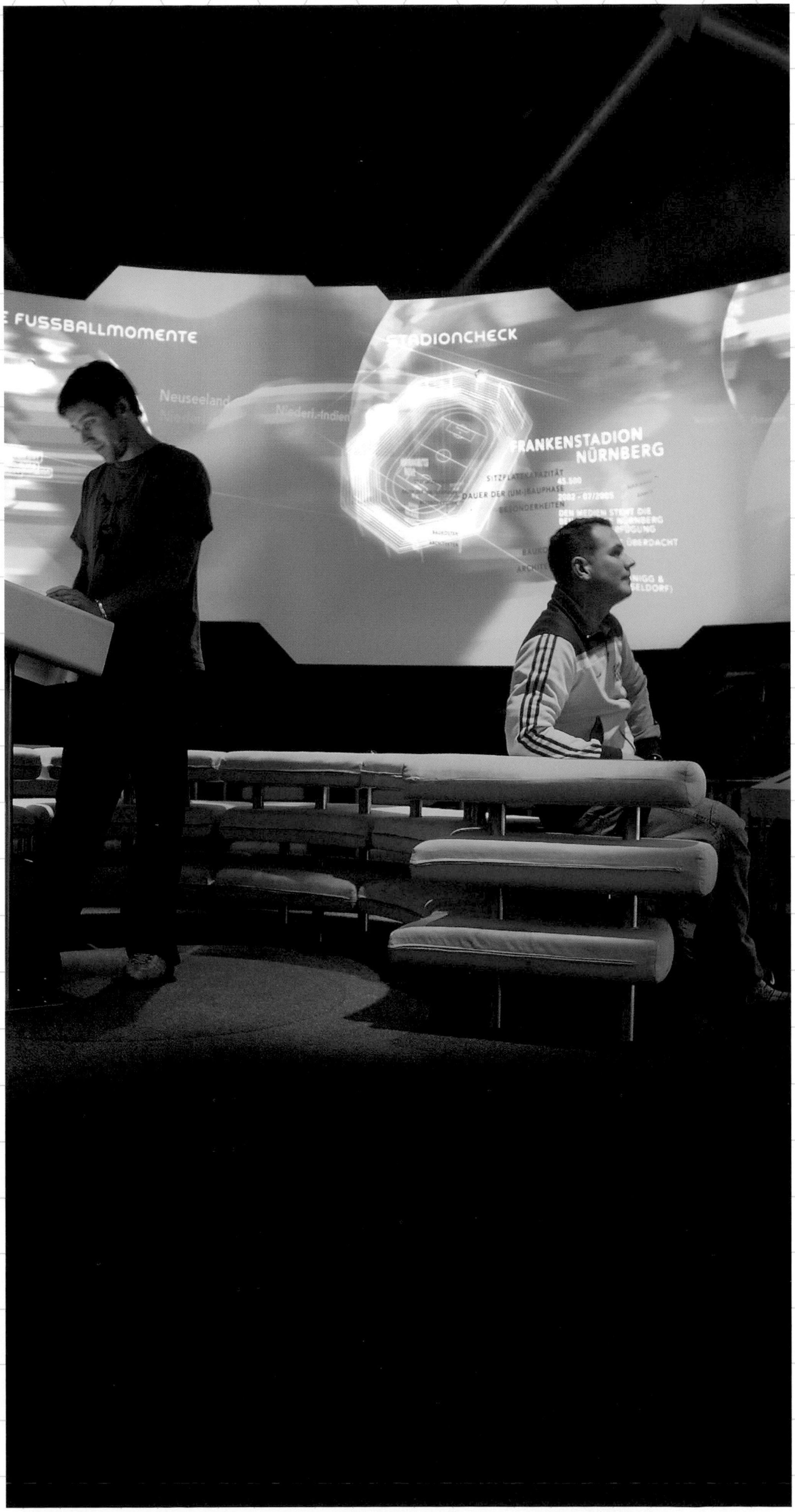

This page: The larger globe made the rounds at home in Germany, appealing to the country's citizens to show their support for the World Cup.

Below, middle and bottom: Accompanying the smaller globe were a camera and touch screens, which encouraged passers-by to perform 'corner flag dances'.

Joga 3 street football is played by two teams of three players; each match is three minutes long.

NIKE BRAND DESIGN
JOGA BONITO
AMSTERDAM, NETHERLANDS

Kick It With a Swoosh

This summer, over 2 million Joga 3 games were played across 39 countries, involving more than 2.5 million players. Joga 3 was Nike's global tournament celebrating football in 2006. Taking its name from the phrase 'joga bonito', Portuguese for 'play beautifully', the tournament was inspired by Futsal, the football game credited with honing the magic of Brazilian Football. Joga 3 is played with a futsal ball, a smaller and heavier ball than the traditional football. The goals are also smaller, helping encourage the development of players' technical skills such as impressive pannas, deceptive feints, passing and of course the scoring. Games run over a period of three minutes, where two teams of three (3v3) try to outclass their opponents to become the king or queen of the pitch in their own city or community. There is no off-side rule, the only requirement is to showcase your pace, wit, skills and tricks.
The Joga 3 tournament was directly linked to the Nikefootball.com website. 'Nike and Google have given people everywhere the chance to create their own global community dedicated to their shared passion for football,' said Trevor Edwards, Nike's vice president of global brand management. 'We created the destination and tools. Now it's up to people who love the beautiful game to log on, sign up and build a community that celebrates brilliant football and the joy of playing the world's most popular sport.'
The event, an offshoot of Nike's international Joga Bonita campaign – the biggest street-football tournament in the world – had a number of interpretations. The German Joga 3 Arena was in a castle, the UK had theirs in Highbury Stadium and the Dutch created a venue drenched in Brazilian atmosphere. All Joga 3 tournaments had a distinctly urban feel and flavour with the grass being replaced by city squares and comparatively 'underground' locations where players could showcase their football wizardry.

Kubik created the football pitch out of weather-beaten containers stacked at random.

In order to allow as many people as possible to experience the Joga 3 games, the pitches were designed to be mobile: unloaded, set up, taken down and loaded back into trucks in a matter of hours. Perimeter fences were constructed from pond lining, a strong woven fabric that unrolled easily and withstood the force of hundreds of footballs per hour. Additional elements such as vehicle graphics, banner stands, stages, registration 'huts' and signage elements were provided to allow each country to create an impactful event and customize the event grounds to a particular location and size of event. Nike's European Brand Design also established a visual look and feel for the country finals to ensure brand consistency and impact.

The design of the pitch in Amsterdam was lead by Nike's European Brand Design team in collaboration with Springtime and Kubik. The pitch was built using locally available materials and was quick and easy to assemble. The site, at one end of Java, an island in the IJ Lake, is connected to the city of Amsterdam by bridge. The basic elements of the design were sea containers. The Joga 3 football arena was created by randomly stacking the weather-beaten containers – deliberately selected for their colour, holes and rust spots. They were all welded together and weighted with 40,000 litres of water. The audience could oversee the field from the resulting stands. Discarded American school buses scattered over the grounds doubled as 'display cases' apparently disgorged from sea containers. Nike's European and Global Brand Design group developed the tournament's graphic look and feel, inspired by Brazilian street art with ingredients of the design inspired by Brazilian people and culture: favelas, beaches, capoeira, samba and futevôlei. They designed huge, easily removable vinyl graphics, which looked as if they were sprayed on and even had imitation 'halos' like the ones you get with spray cans. The tournament's values were expressed by a 'football manifesto', signed by professional football players, and by using five crests inscribed with the game's values: honour, joy, skill, team and heart. Crests were displayed in each corner of the pitch and were supported by imagery of the athletes who subscribed to the manifesto. Regional tournament winners were also celebrated through the use of posters carrying the images of local winners.

Along with the title of national champions, all country winners have won the prize to travel to Rio de Janeiro, the home of the 'Joga Bonito' game, where they will play each other, visit the headquarters of the Brazilian National team and attend a top division game in the famous Maracana stadium to complete their Nikefootball experience. Goal!

The tournament's graphic look and feel was inspired by Brazilian street art.

Designer: Nike Brand Design – www.nike.com
Photographer: Fridtjof Versnel – T +31 20 6132 335

Client: Nike Inc. – www.nike.com
Consultants: Kubik (environmental setup), Springtime (mobile-court design)
Engineers: Arno Fords (mobile courts), Kubik (container setup)
Manufacturers: Arno Fords
Start of event: April 2006

Images of athletes associated with the Joga Bonito project were displayed at each corner of the pitch.

HONOR

This page and opposite: Nike's Global Brand Design developed the graphic look of the Joga Bonito tournament – a design concept inspired by Brazilian street art.

NIKEFOOTBALL.COM

SKILLS ARE
YOUR WEAPONS
POLISH THEM
DAILY.
APRIL

NIKEFOOTBALL
NIKEFOOTBALL.COM
JOY
PITCH 1

Always on the move, the Heineken 'greenspace' project offers a platform for the work of young adults involved in music, film and design.

ADRIAN CADDY AND MIKE KETTLES
HEINEKEN GREENSPACE
VALENCIA, SPAIN

Beyond the Norm

Firms that develop concepts for products and that profile brands increasingly use so-called 'soft skills'. They belong to a category of businesses that combine creative and market-orientated services (furnished by in-house or external facilities), such as design, architecture, photography, advertising, film and multimedia. In the development of a product concept or a unique corporate profile, such resources can make a significant contribution to the success of the project. This may explain why Heineken, the International brewery behind the 'greenspace' project, is offering young adults from the fields of music, film and design a broad platform for their work – projects geared to Heineken's belief that 'new and rewarding experiences can be had by going beyond the norm'. Taking its platform seriously, Heineken is supporting emerging talent while also using greenspace to stimulate urban development and to provide new kinds of cultural meeting points.

Heineken used design to embed its brand to connect with key opinion leaders. 'In the process of curating greenspace, we assembled buildings, people, projects, exhibitions and events in order to bring to life the Heineken philosophy as a simple story with which interested visitors could empathize and engage,' says Adrian Caddy who along with Mike Kettles are the creative directors of greenspace. 'The philosophy in question is a point of view that we concurred with at the outset of the project.' Since 2003, Adrian Caddy, Mike Kettles and the Heineken greenspace team have been on a worldwide search for locations with no history of hosting major events but with a sure potential for attracting a young target group. Mobile units capable of moving from venue to venue are a major part of the project.

The Heineken greenspace team decided on specially adapted sea containers for these units, with an eye to creating an appealingly youthful atmosphere.

The greenspace event in Valencia transformed an old harbour site into a cultural meeting point.

'We came up with the idea of a touring urban village,' says Caddy, 'and because the containers are emblematic of the Heineken brand, we called it "greenspace". They form what looks like a small village, where creative activities like film, music and design are the core experience.'

The greenspace event in Valencia, held in October 2005, marked the start of a series of Heineken-sponsored happenings 'aimed at investing in the urban cultures of cities worldwide', as stated on the website. The organizers had identified Valencia as a city that had not quite made its mark on the cultural map of the world, but which had huge potential. They quickly found the ideal site: a number of grain stores that had lain empty for a decade or more and were just begging to be developed.

An added advantage was the choice of Valencia to host the famous sailing competition, the America's Cup, in 2007. To brush up the city's image, municipal authorities welcomed a building initiative at an unused site near the harbour.

'When we approached the council to explain our ideas,' says Caddy, 'they became very interested in the possibilities of a longer-term partnership. It was at this point that we found the derelict warehouses near the port that would become the venue.'

Ultimately, the buildings were lavishly restored, but to begin with they had to be rendered safe for future visitors. Roofs were renovated and windows and doors repaired or replaced. Also renewed were all water, sewage and electricity systems throughout the 5000-m² area. Having reached that stage of the restoration, the team was able to install mobile greenspace containers inside and outside the buildings. These units would not only house the necessary audiovisual equipment, but would also function as supplementary exhibition areas and stages.

Running parallel to the search for a location and its development is the selection of content for the event and its realization. In Valencia, Heineken launched a competition for Spanish designers, musicians and filmmakers between the ages of 18 and 35, who were asked to submit unusual ideas for projects. Ten to 12 finalists from the three disciplines were invited to develop their ideas with the support of internationally recognized mentors. The winning results were presented at a week-long greenspace festival. Mentors were OMA founder Rem Koolhaas (design and architecture), musician and producer Matthew Herbert (music) and Spanish director Santiago Tabernero and his team (film). After the kick-off, the warehouses were used by Heineken for another six months as the venue for cultural events. During this time, restoration of the buildings continued. The final completion of the site and its handover to the city are planned for 2007, in time for the start of the America's Cup. Afterwards, the area will continue to be used for cultural events. In the meantime, the Heineken caravan will move on. As this book goes to press, the search is on for a location for the second greenspace event. Again with the same recyclable containers and again with the cream of a youthful crop of local talent in the fields of film, design and music.

They quickly found the ideal site: a number of grain stores that had lain empty for a decade or more and were just begging to be developed.

Creative direction: Adrian Caddy and Mike Kettles – www.thegreenspace.com
Photographers: Alex James – www.alexjamesphotography.com
Tom Oldham – www.tomoldham.com

Environmental design: Brinkworth Design
Exhibition design: Samir Bantal, OMA, Lomography
Public Relations: piranhaKid
Exhibition curators: Dorothee Gaeta and Jordan Mirchev
Graphic design: Small Studio
Audiovisual consultant: CC Lab
Engineer: Nova Ingenieria
Manufacturers: Wren Marine, Suite 347
Capacity: 3500 guests
Total floor area (m²): 5000
Duration of construction: 8 months
Start of event: 24 October 2005

This page and opposite: Reconstruction of the site provided the city of Valencia with a week-long greenspace festival, complete with music, design and film.

This page and opposite: Reusable, mobile containers held audiovisual equipment and served as exhibition spaces and stages.

greenspace
cotidiano
delirio
hyperstreet 23
greenissimo
green box sessions
minibar
movument
nbz - no brand zone
nktorn
piérdete project
EXTINTOR
AJUNTAMENT DE VALENCIA
REGIDORIA DE JOVENTUT

Built for Versailles Off, part of an annual event in Paris known as Les Nuits Blanches, the colossal disco ball suddenly found itself among highly unusual surroundings.

Text by Chris Scott

AGENCE PATRICK JOUIN
DISCOTHÈQUE FOR VERSAILLES OFF
PARIS, FRANCE

Dancing Under the Sun

Les Nuits Blanches, an annual event in Paris, takes places over several nights in the late summer. This cultural happening – in and around the city – attracts crowds of visitors. Versailles Off, which is part of the festival, is staged in the vast gardens of the royal palace of Versailles. In 2005 a number of artists and one designer, Patrick Jouin, were given carte blanche to create an object or installation for Versailles Off.

Jouin's initial visit to Versailles to select a spot for his work was on a winter's day, when everything was covered in snow and no visitors were to be seen. It was a situation in total contrast to the final spectacle, which would happen late at night and attract thousands of spectators. His eye fell on a delightful theatre encircled by a grove. It was in these surroundings that, approximately three hundred years ago, Louis XIV had held his grandes fêtes, extravagant galas that testified to his power and wealth. Jouin's initial thought was to 'make a party' that would show the royal ghost that Versailles now welcomes all citizens of France and of countries worldwide.

The circumstances surrounding this event were quite different from those marking most of Jouin's other, often long-term, projects. Here his work would exist for only one night. (In reality, it remained in place for three nights.) 'It's always about emotions, whatever the project,' says Jouin. Underlining his words are the restaurants he designs, interiors in which he attempts to stimulate and sustain a certain mood for several hours. But here at Versailles, the aim was a short, sharp emotive burst meant to entertain observers for, say, ten minutes tops.

Visitors would pass through Versailles Off, going from emotion to emotion, observing and experiencing a series of events. Jouin's contribution, which was to follow a striking creation by artist Daniel Buren, had to be strong, simple and independent.

Crowds flocked to view the rotating orb, which the designer compared to a sunset.

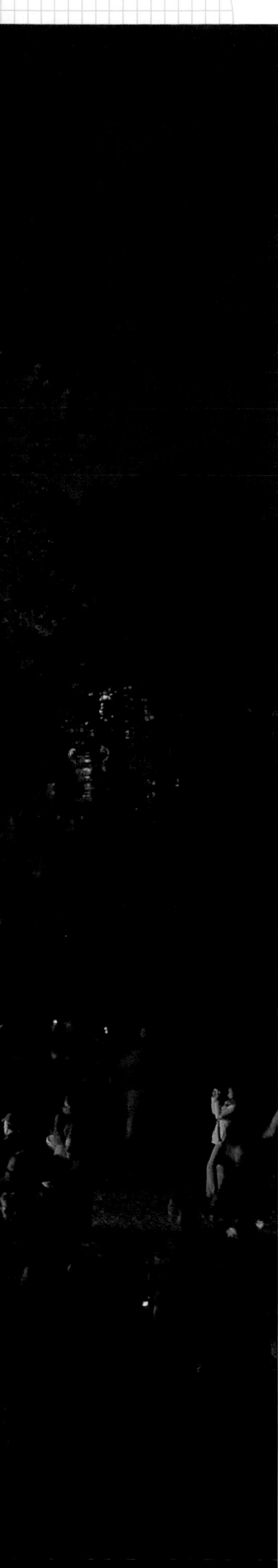

What better exemplified his party concept than a disco ball? Not just any disco ball, of course, but one that would measure 6 m in diameter: the biggest ever made. The ideal solution, in terms of both weight and budget, was an inflatable balloon. This party balloon, however, sent the scale soaring to 239 kg!

A constant stream of air kept the orb inflated, and it rotated slowly, thanks to a motorized mechanism. The multifaceted surface boasted 4914 gold-toned aluminium mirrors, each glued to the ball by hand, prior to and after inflation. It took a month to complete. 'A simple but very effective object. No high-tech solutions,' Jouin remarks. 'As architects, we know how to find solutions. We simply worked out the effect we wanted.'

Enhancing the project was a typical French play on words. Louis XIV was called Le Roi-Soleil (the Sun King), and the disco ball resembled a huge sun. Jouin loved the idea of this 'tacky, but stunning object'. Light reflecting on the enormous rotating ball produced an awesome sight that Jouin compares to a sunset. 'It was just beautiful,' he enthuses.

Although the ball was Jouin's idea, the project was realized through close collaboration with lighting specialist Dominique Breemersch and DJ Krikor Kouchian. All three were vital players in 'the show'. Appropriate music accompanied the event: a mix of contemporary electronic sounds and music from the period of Louis XIV. From his DJ box, a location surrounded by fountains that is the exact spot used by musicians in the golden olden days, Krikor gave visitors his best performance on the night in question.

To reach the disco ball, visitors first passed through a wooded area in which DJ Krikor's music could be faintly heard. As they approached the setting, the sounds grew increasingly louder, and when the amphitheatre became visible, the magnificent ball suddenly exploded into view. Voila! It was a magical experience, like finding a hidden treasure. The look on each visitor's face was Jouin's reward. 'When you see people smile, you know something good is happening,' he says. At least 20,000 people and 20,000 smiles joined his creation in illuminating the darkness. Next day, all was gone, like a dream that had vanished in the night, leaving a wonderful souvenir and the memory of having witnessed Versailles in a very different light.

An event poetically summed up by Jouin:

'*Une nuit blanche à Versailles,*
un jardin, un bosquet : La salle de Bal.
Nous dansons une carmagnole électronique
autour d'un soleil doré.
Dans notre jardin, citoyen!
Le Roi savait s'amuser.
Profitons-en.'

'A white night at Versailles,
a garden, a grove: the ballroom.
We dance the electronic carmagnole around a gilded sun.
In our garden, citizens!
The King knew how to amuse himself.
Let us also enjoy it.'

'As architects, we know how to find solutions.
We simply worked out the effect we wanted.' Patrick Jouin

Designer: Agence Patrick Jouin – www.patrickjouin.com
Photographer: J.M. Manaï

Client: Versailles Off – julie.beret@chateauversailles.fr
Lighting consultant: Dominique Breemersh
Sound creator: Krikor Kouchian
Manufacturer: Audio Scène
Manufacturers: Créatonaute, Johan Brunel and Audio Scène
Start of event: 1 October 2005

Below left and bottom left: Construction of the huge ball.
Below right, bottom and opposite: Lighting and music generated an intriguing range of effects and moods that continued throughout the night.

An amphitheatre in a grove in Versailles was chosen as the location for the enormous globe, which revolved slowly, illuminating the woodland scene around it.

In response to conventional 'uptight' gallery presentations, Amsterdam-based Featuring transformed the opening of ArtOlive Young Talent 2005 into a lively happening for an art-loving public.

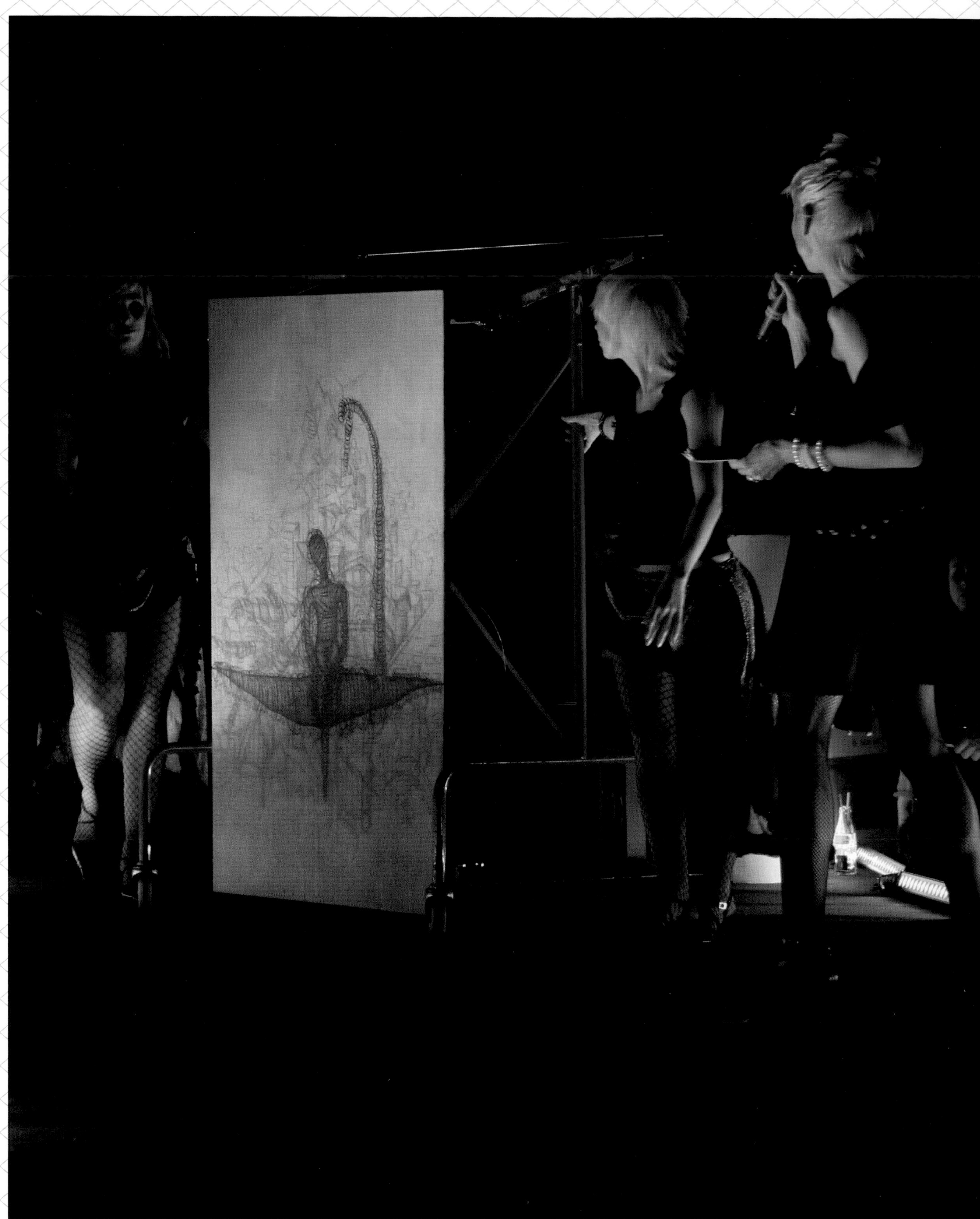

FEATURING
ARTOLIVE YOUNG TALENT 2005
AMSTERDAM, NETHERLANDS

Catwalk Art

Amsterdam art-rental company ArtOlive organizes an annual competition to find the most promising graduate of a Dutch art academy. When ArtOlive moved to the grounds of the Westergasfabriek (Wester Gasworks), a former industrial complex not far from central Amsterdam, the exhibition accompanying the competition moved there too. In 2005 the design of the three-day show, which revolved around the work of 36 creatives, was entrusted to local firm Featuring. Opting for an unconventional approach, Featuring opened the event with a lively presentation much like a fashion show. A well-known Dutch VJ added extra sparkle to the spectacle.
Featuring is a multidisciplinary design studio consisting of an architect (Michl Sommer), a designer (Victor Leurs) and a concept developer (Cyril Chermin). Their portfolio includes Europan 7 Rotterdam, an assisted-living accommodation for elderly; VU Kinderstad, an entertainment centre for ill children that fills the roof of a hospital; and Unexposed, an interactive exhibition installation (featured in *Frame* 46) and ArtBank, a multifunctional art display/loungechair for an art rental company. Previous experience with trade-fair stands and art exhibitions helped them land the commission for ArtOlive Young Talent 2005.
The job represented a whopping challenge. Besides all the art to be displayed and the oh-so-tight budget of € 7000, Westergasfabriek's former purifying house is a 1200-m^2 space that holds about 2000 people. Cyril Chermin of Featuring: 'Whatever concept we chose to carry out, it clearly had to fill the massive space involved. It's an enormous hall, and there was no way to estimate how many people would turn up to see the exhibition. Anything we designed would have to fill the massive hall and make it feel more alive.'

By concentrating all works of art on a 70-m-long 'wall of exhibition', the designers managed to focus every eye in the enormous factory hall on the reason for the event.

The solution was aimed at putting the exhibition in an innovative context, for both artist and public. Although the nominated work included paintings, graphic art, sculpture and audiovisual installations, most of it was two-dimensional. Consequently, Featuring grouped all 200 works on one 70-m-long wall, placing them close to one another as was the custom in 19th-century museums. 'The result was an impressive image and a clear focal point within the immense hall,' says Chermin.

The limited budget forced them to leave the rest of the interior as it was. They did nothing to conceal the original features of the factory. The industrial feel of the space actually enhanced the exciting underground nature of the exhibition. Given an entirely new function in the 1990s, the revitalized gasworks has since evolved into a cultural village for film, theatre and art. A diversity of creative industries and hospitality facilities have found a permanent home here, and temporary events include festivals, performances and the making of films. The former purifying house, with its elongated shape, is especially suitable for fairs and large exhibitions.

The design for ArtOlive Young Talent 2005 did not begin and end with a wall-mounted display of art. Fronting the wall was a 40-m-long catwalk: a stage to be used for highlighting the achievements of individual artists during the opening. In playing up the 'show' element of 'art show', Featuring had hit on the device for generating interaction between artists and visitors and create a visual contrast between the individual pieces of art and the group exhibition. Some artwork was carried by the artists and by 'air hostesses'; other pieces were moved along the catwalk on wheeled clothing racks. This ludicrous method of presentation, says Chermin, was a response to conventional, 'uptight' gallery shows. 'Each piece was part of a group exhibition, but moving along the catwalk, it was on its own.' After all the work had been introduced, the winner was announced and given the Green ArtOlive Award.

Although the idea of artists as models recalls performances from the '70s, Chermin says it was based mainly on practical considerations. 'We were quite keen to engage the artists in the show and to present both the work and its maker to the audience. We think it's an important part of this type of event.' 'Art hostesses' paraded around in provocative get-ups: think bustiers, ruches, fishnet stockings. 'These outfits were a more respectable version of those worn by ring girls at boxing matches,' says Chermin. 'The idea was a tongue-in-cheek comment on the predominantly elitist character of art.'

The vitality of the show was boosted by special lighting effects designed by Micha Klein – top VJ and computer artist – in collaboration with lighting firm Maas Licht & Geluid. 'The lighting could be regulated per metre, which allowed us to create a shifting point of interest,' explains Chermin. Klein was also responsible for dazzling pre- and post-show audiovisuals.

Looking back, Chermin recalls few glitches, thanks in particular to the close cooperation between Featuring and ArtOlive. 'The only stumbling block was one artist who didn't like the setup and refused to participate. And a bigger budget would have paid for a few extra finishing touches. Generally speaking, however, the concept was well implemented.' In the end, the client's brief was satisfied: ArtOlive Young Talent 2005 swept art into motion, while turning its back on the traditional and rather arrogant image of art-related events.

'Anything we designed would have to fill the massive hall and make it feel more alive.' Cyril Chermin

Designer: Featuring – www.featuring-amsterdam.nl
Photographer: Pieter Claessen – www.pieterclaessen.com
Gaudi Houdaya – www.suite17.nl

Client: ArtOlive – www.galerie.nl
Consultants: Micha Klein, Maas Licht & Geluid
Manufacturer: Maas Licht & Geluid
Capacity: 2000 guests
Total floor area (m²): 1200
Total cost (€): 7000
Start of event: 11 November 2005

This page and opposite: Models show the work of the graduated students on a 40-m-long catwalk.

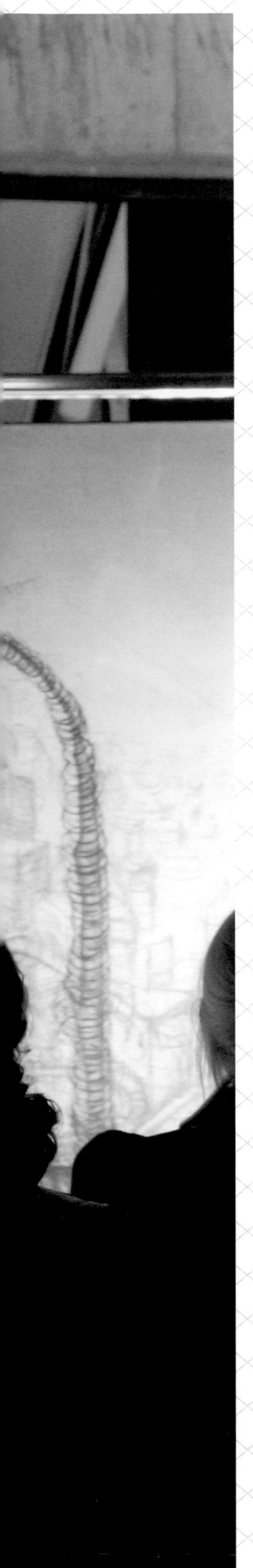

This page and opposite: Featuring used the 'show' concept to get both artists and guests involved in the exhibition.

Below left: Ashley Ramage of Blowupthings UK stretched white fabric covers over 200 chairs arranged in rows.

Text by Sarah Martín Pearson

BLOWUPTHINGS
VOK DAMS GALA AWARD
CHICAGO, ILLINOIS, USA

Surprise!

It was up to Ashley Ramage of Blowupthings to create a setting for what Vok Dams North America calls its Gala Award. Picturing an event that would surprise the audience, the experiential-marketing firm was particularly interested in Blowupthings' collection of inflatables, most of which have been made to furnish temporary interiors. The award ceremony, held in a function room at the Chicago Marriot, had to accommodate some 200 seated guests. Ramage stretched white fabric covers over 200 chairs arranged in rows. Placed on each chair was a brightly coloured cardboard box, shaped like a pyramid, containing information about the event. At the close of the ceremony, the challenge was to move everyone out of their seats and into a rear area screened off from the rest of the space by a wall composed of inflatable segments, each of which weighed 12 kg and featured built-in lighting. Easy to assemble, dismantle and shift from one spot to another, these building-block modules were moved aside to allow people to pass through and then reassembled to hide from view what was happening in the area they had just vacated. Having been herded behind the wall, guests found themselves in a space with a bar, where they enjoyed drinks and canapés for 35 minutes while awaiting the following surprise. During this short interval, the 'auditorium' used for the award ceremony was transformed into a chill-out lounge, complete with different furniture, tables with built-in lighting, bottles of champagne in ice buckets, large inflatable structures and a clear message: 'Let the party begin!'

The chill-out zone was organized around a series of inflatable structures resembling halved igloos.

The guests were amazed at the rapid conversion of the rather formally arranged part of the room, where rows of chairs had been packed as tightly as economy-class seats in a passenger plane, with little room for knees and elbows, into a lounge with ample space for circulating and socializing in a more relaxing environment. Highlighting the scene were dancers in futuristic white costumes composed of large cell-shaped layers that made their performance absolutely dynamic as they whirled across the floor. Blowupthings had injected amusement and visual stimulation into an interior that had a pleasingly aesthetic impact on Vok Dams' guests.

The chill-out zone was organized around a series of inflatable structures resembling halved igloos or what Americans call 'band shells'. A continuous and silent stream of air from a blower kept the ice caves structures inflated, and built-in multicoloured LEDs gave them a festive glow. Ramage reveals that the inflatables 'are made of flame-retardant nylon fabric' and that they sit 'flat on the floor thanks to a clear, corrugated-plastic base' that houses the light source'. When asked why the objects do not come in a range of colours, he says that 'white is like a canvas over which you can apply a palette of coloured light. The result is stunning. I'm all about visual impact.'

The ice caves objects used for this particular event unfolded like the hoods of convertible cars to form cosy corners that invited people to congregate around them, adding to the enjoyment of the casual party ambience. Ramage says that one effect of Blowupthings is that 'people want to be in a space that is this inviting, engaging and soft'. He customized the gala inflatables by modifying their semicircular shape to generate more of the 'shell feeling' he hoped would give guests a sense of being embraced by the structures. The resulting shelters accommodated a fair number of people without making those outside feel excluded.

In the halved igloos and scattered throughout the space was aluminium-framed furniture clad in white vinyl upholstery; these pieces included triangular poufs and low, round tables with polycarbonate tops and built-in lighting. Serpentine seating in the form of a long bench composed of modular units shared the centre of the room with round tables and L-shaped sofas wrapped around small elevated corner tables, again with built-in lighting, for drinks.

The fantastical structures made possible with inflatables allow the designer total flexibility in the creation and re-creation of space. Not only do they adapt to all types of indoor and outdoor locations; they also transform the venue involved into something brand new with the utmost speed and simplicity. Upgrading these benefits at the Vok Dams Gala Award were the element of surprise, the visible impact of Blowupthings on the guests, and the presence of ice cave structures, which added to the cosy, convivial atmosphere. 'Providing everyone with a "little home" in which to gather,' says Ramage, 'rather than having guests huddle in a cramped seating area, allowed people to relax and interact more freely. The success of the overall event, however, was really about combining all elements to form a whole that worked together to produce the desired impression.'

'I'm all about visual impact.' Ashley Ramage

Designer: Blowupthings – www.blowupthings.com
Photographer: Padgett & Co – www.padgettandco.com

Client: Event Marketer Magazine
Production: Vok Dams North America – www.vokdams.com
Capacity: 200 guests
Duration of construction: 1 day (first set up), 35 minutes (second set up)
Start of event: April 2005

This page and opposite: A continuous and silent stream of air from a blower kept the structures inflated, and built-in multicoloured LEDs gave them a festive glow.

This page and opposite: Futuristic white costumes composed of large cell-shaped layers made the dancers' performance absolutely dynamic as they whirled across the floor.

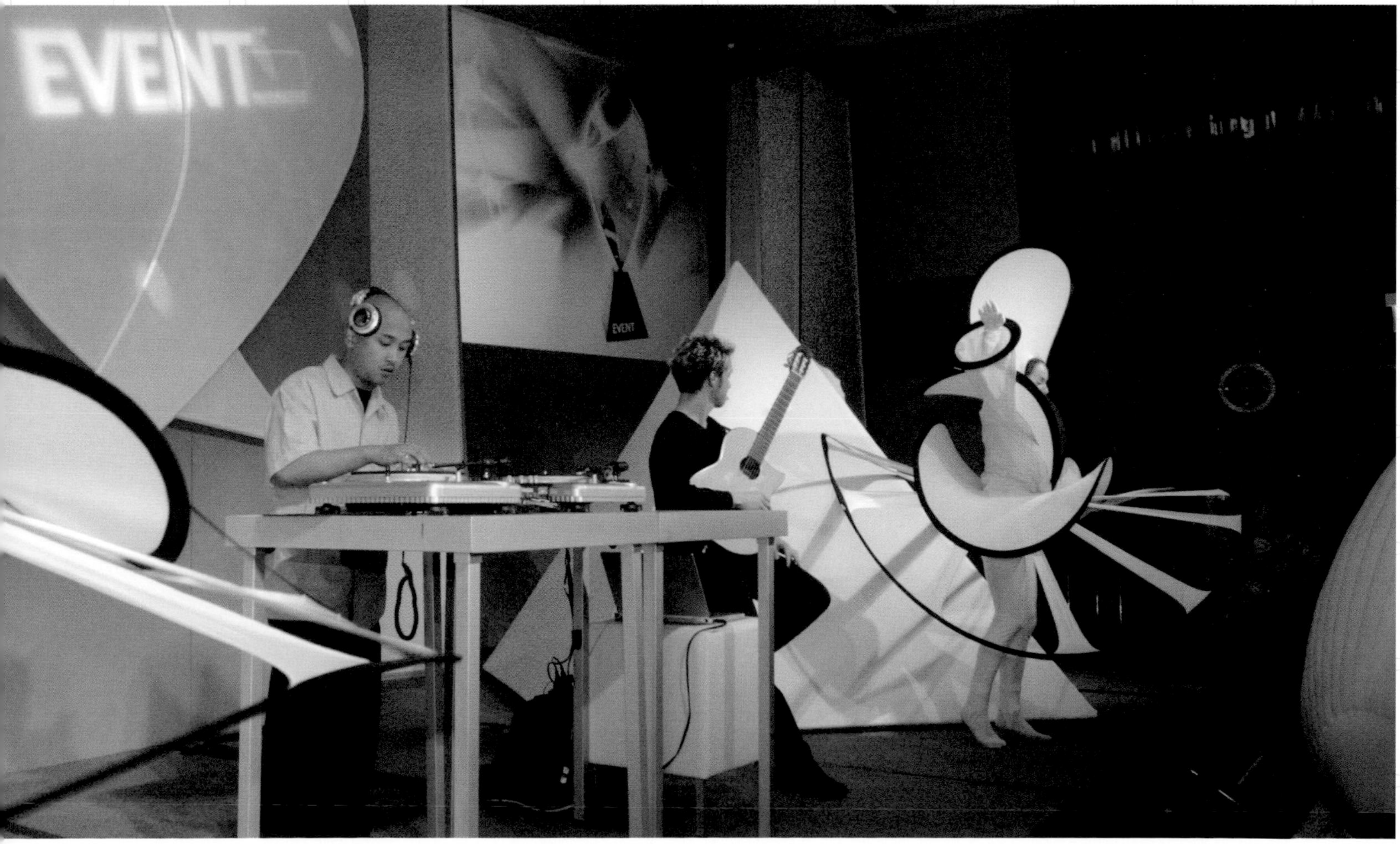

A screen on the Ferris wheel transformed the promenade into an open-air cinema.

ATELIER MARKGRAPH
MUSEUM RIVERBANK FESTIVALS
FRANKFURT, GERMANY

Main Event

Following World War II, Frankfurt nearly became the capital of the new Federal Republic of Germany, but Chancellor Adenauer wanted politics situated in Bonn, which was home to the seat of government until reunification was established years later. A stroke of luck for Frankfurt, you might say, for when the capital moved to Berlin in 1999, a hush settled over Bonn, whereas the intervening decades had turned Frankfurt into a major centre of trade, banking and transport. No abandoned ministries on the skyline of Frankfurt, but a high-rise forest of international banks, including the European Central Bank. Other landmarks are the Frankfurt Messe, a world-renowned trade-fair centre, and Frankfurt Airport, which handles more cargo than any other European airport.

The River Main, along whose banks the first medieval traders settled, is no longer a significant trade and transportation route for Frankfurt. In the mid-1980s, municipal authorities began developing the south bank of the Main by turning vacant 19th-century villas into museums. Every summer since 1987, the city has held the Museum Riverbank Festival: a bridge to inner-city museums and an event meant to draw more visitors to the south bank. Funfairs lining both sides of the river feature 'lucky buttons' that entitle winners to free museum visits.

Every year the festival attracts some three million people from all over the world. But ties between the festival and the city's museums were vanishing quickly, says Roland Lambrette, co-founder and head of Atelier Markgraph. In 2002 the organizers of the Festival, Tourismus+Congress Frankfurt am Main, called on Lambrette's agency for a solution. Every year since then Atelier Markgraph has focused public awareness squarely on the 16 museums in question, while also emphasizing the importance of the river to the city's identity. The Frankfurter creatives work primarily with projected images and film sequences.

40 high-performance projectors casted moving pictures onto the façades.

Their 2003 'SHIP OF IDEAS', pulled by a tug, glided down the river after dark. It was 23 m long and equipped with broad screens and LED's on the port. As it passed each museum, projected images showed items from that museum's collection. The speed of the boat and the length of the film sequence were coordinated. Images appeared at the exact height of each museum; the vessel seemed to be scanning the hidden contents and revealing what was found inside.

The following year the Markgraph team under the direction of Lambrette displayed an installation on the lower Main Bridge. The commuter route, now closed to traffic, became an open-air cinema: SOUND | PASSAGES. Two screens lined the bridge, and on both sides little flags suspended from three ropes hung one above the other. The flags doubled as projection screens. RGB lights beneath the fabric were programmed to heighten the film sequences. A 25-minute, acoustically enhanced loop featuring Frankfurt musicians referred to the motto of the festival: 'Music in Art and Art in Music'. Viewers watched the media show from the banks or walked right through it.

In 2005 Atelier Markgraph incorporated the Frankfurt skyline into its concept. The skyscrapers, while characteristic of the city, are in daily life unappreciated by many residents. To change their minds, Lambrette persuaded a Ferris-wheel operator to join the festivities. Set up along the bank, the 40-m-high wheel wore a meshed scaffolding tarpaulin, which gave the wheel a circular screen, wonderfully in tune with the globular World Culture/Cultural World theme of the festival. Each gondola on the wheel related to a particular museum. When a museum was indicated by a randomly generated Cursor, a sequence of animated pictures from the respective museum would begin, running in sync with the wheel. From their perches high above the riverbank, visitors viewed river, festivities and city as a romantic entity.

Lambrette, who grew up in a Frankfurt heavily damaged by war, wants these events to strengthen the city's image, which many feel is rather cold. He believes that Frankfurters are warming to their city and its history, which is marked by a willingness to embrace change. He points to the ever-increasing high-rises as creators of Frankfurt's identity and as a sign of the city's faith in the future.

It seemed only natural to give the high-rises an even greater role in the next production. Lambrette pulled out a plan he'd made in 2001 to introduce the Euro, but was canceled because of 11 September – a design that would imbue the skyline with an emotional story. It took five years and the 2006 FIFA World Cup, hosted by Germany, to reach completion. The museum riverbank became the auditorium and the skyline the stage set, with 40 high-performance projectors casting moving pictures onto the façades. Called SkyArena, the event had an original soundtrack that was transmitted by radio, and images of the festival were seen on television by viewers worldwide. SkyArena brought Atelier Markgraph one step closer to the goal of 'branding' its home city.

The museum riverbank became the auditorium and the skyline of Frankfurt the stage set.

Creative Direction: Roland Lambrette (SHIP OF IDEAS, SOUND | PASSAGES, ART | WHEEL, SkyArena), Stefan Weil (ART | WHEEL, SkyArena).
Art Direction: Alexander Hanowski (SkyArena), Eno Henze (SHIP OF IDEAS), Andreas Lorenschat (SHIP OF IDEAS, SOUND | PASSAGES), Jan Schmelter (ART | WHEEL), Kristin Trümper (ART | WHEEL).
Design: Atelier Markgraph – www.markgraph.de
Photographers: Cem Yücetas – www.cemyuecetas.de, Katja Hoffmann – www.katjahoffmann.de, Markus Becker – www.idee-und-raum.de, Ralph Larmann – www.rlcompany.de, Amir Molana – www.amirmolana.net

Client: Tourismus+Congress Frankfurt am Main – www.tcf.frankfurt.de
Construction, lighting and sound: Procon Multimedia (SHIP OF IDEAS, SOUND | PASSAGES, ART | WHEEL), Nüssli Deutschland (construction SkyArena), Media Spektrum (sound SkyArena) and Satis&Fy (lighting SkyArena).
Video technology: XL Video (SHIP OF IDEAS, SOUND/PASSAGES, ART | WHEEL), Velten GmbH (ART | WHEEL) and XXL Vision (SkyArena).
Lighting design: Dietrich Körner (ART | WHEEL) & Gunther Hecker (SkyArena).
Digital Media System Design: Meso (SHIP OF IDEAS, SOUND | PASSAGES, ART | WHEEL).
Animation and picture: m box (SkyArena).
Sound design: Parviz Mir-Ali (SHIP OF IDEAS, SOUND | PASSAGES, SKYARENA) and Ole Schulte (ART | WHEEL).
Start of event: 29 August 2003 (SHIP OF IDEAS), 27 August 2004 (SOUND | PASSAGES), 26 August 2005 (ART | WHEEL), 3 June 2006 (SkyArena)

This page and opposite: SkyArena was an event that relied on the identifying effect of architecture.

Top and opposite top: Each gondola on the wheel related to a particular museum.
Bottom and opposite bottom: The Museum Riverbank Festival 2003 featured a ship as a projection surface.

An entrance featuring gigantic wooden letters lent access to De Balie, a venue at Amsterdam's Cinekid Film Festival that invited children to test CD-ROMs, computer games and websites.

MARCEL SCHMALGEMEIJER
CINEKID FILM FESTIVAL
AMSTERDAM, NETHERLANDS

Now I Know My ABC's

During the annual Cinekid festival that takes place in De Balie and Pathé City in Amsterdam, kindergarteners to teenagers watch feature films, TV programmes and documentaries aimed at their specific age groups. The festival includes premieres, interviews, award ceremonies and workshops. A highlight of the 15th edition was an interactive 'digital playground', located in De Balie, where children could test and evaluate the latest CD-ROMs, computer games and websites. Coaxing the kids to participate in this project was not left entirely to chance. Designer Marcel Schmalgemeijer placed a monumental 'gateway' of three-dimensional letters in front of the entrance to De Balie. Punctuating his 18-m-wide alphabet portal was a large circular opening: a dark theatrical hole that drew the public inside the festival building with an almost physical force.

In addition to the main opening, other cutouts perforated the entranceway, each with a distinct function. 'The circular holes and the star-shaped hole,' says the designer, 'brought daylight into the café and hall.' Without his special façade, De Balie's large, high windows offer a direct view of the street. 'But because people inside would see only the new construction when they looked out the window,' continues Schmalgemeijer, 'I clad the glass panes in a coloured film which has the same cutouts that appear in the added volume.'

Marcel Schmalgemeijer attended the Academy of Industrial Design Eindhoven (AIVE) – now Design Academy Eindhoven – where he specialized in the design of open space. From 1994 to 1998, he worked for the Zuidelijk Toneel (Southern Theatre) as the full-time assistant of scenographer and lighting designer Jan Versweyveld. Currently a freelance spatial designer, Schmalgemeijer focuses on theatre (scenography/lighting), exhibitions, public spaces and events. In 2002 he received the Charlotte Köhler Prize, a Dutch incentive award for artists under 35, in the category of theatre design.

Sucked into the festival building as though by magnetic force, visitors entered through a circular hole cut out of the letter-adorned 'gateway'.

Elly Engel, head organizer of Cinekid, asked Schmalgemeijer to create a false façade for De Balie that would leave enough room for pedestrians to pass by and for people to enter the building. 'In terms of materialization, what immediately came to mind was the hoarding around a building site – street language, kids, bravura – but in a deluxe version featuring letters in relief. A 3D hoarding, actually.'

Schmalgemeijer says his use of monumental letters has its roots in illuminated advertising and other outdoor signage. 'I was inspired by the landmark Hollywood Sign and by brands advertised in capital letters – City, Drum, Heineken and so on – that crown the buildings in the vicinity of De Balie.'

Playing with letters and with two- and three-dimensional typography is typical of Schmalgemeijer's work. For the Impakt Festival of 2001 in Utrecht's Centraal Museum, he used large words and characters as signage. And the 'legs' of the letters that make up his sign for the Amsterdam City Theatre begin above the door and turn the corner in lines of varying widths, like a bar code.

The concept-to-realization process for De Balie can be compared to fitting together the pieces of a jigsaw puzzle. 'First I made a 1:50 scale model out of cardboard. I drew a frontal elevation and divided the whole into components that fit together. Precisely measured letters were produced as volumes by a manufacturer of stage sets. They scaled up the letters in the old-fashioned way on graph paper.' The various components were preassembled and pieced together on site in two days.

The construction – a plasterboard-reinforced wooden wall – was anchored to the building. Individual volumes were stacked and screwed to this wall. Plasterboard was added during the final phase for safety reasons. 'The plasterboard wall fills the entire length and height of the space between the building and the wooden letter wall. Were the wood to catch fire, the plaster would keep the blaze from spreading.'

Within the framework of a programme entitled Temporary Small-Scale Visual Arts Projects, the project was financed by the Amsterdam Art Foundation, which also acted as client. 'Soon after the presentation of my design, which got a highly enthusiastic reception, it was obvious that it couldn't be realized for the amount stated in the proposal,' says Schmalgemeijer. The foundation nearly doubled the initial budget of € 11,000. Despite the increase in funds, the relatively tight budget was crucial in the choice of both design and materials. 'I had made letters in a previous design that were not lopped off at the bottom. Here, because rounding them on all sides would have been too expensive, I saved money by modifying the lower section. Consequently, many curves became angles.' Limitations do not always have to be disadvantageous, however, as noted in Schmalgemeijer's conclusion: 'It gave the design a rougher edge, so to speak, which only strengthened my concept.'

'In terms of materialization, what immediately came to mind was the hoarding around a building site – street language, kids, bravura – but in a deluxe version featuring letters in relief. A 3D hoarding, actually.' Marcel Schmalgemeijer

Designer: Marcel Schmalgemeijer – www.marcelschmalgemeijer.nl
Photographers: Marcel Schmalgemeijer – www.marcelschmalgemeijer.nl, Gert Jan van Rooij

Client: Amsterdams Fonds voor de Kunst – www.amsterdamsfondsvoordekunst.nl
Manufacturer: Joepies decorbouw
Total floor area (m^2): 27
Total cost (€): 20,450
Duration of construction: 2 days
Start of event: 21 October 2001

The three-dimensional hoarding that Schmalgemeijer created to indicate the name of the festival masked the historical façade of De Balie.

This page and opposite: Certain cutouts in the 'alphabetical' entranceway drew natural light into the interior. Those inside saw a surface clad in coloured film rather than the raw construction underneath.

Inside the box, visitors enjoy the powerful taste and energy-generating experience promised by Burn.

STOREAGE
BURN BLACK BOX

Burning the Midnight Flame

Enormous, enigmatic black cubes are appearing in major metropolitan centres – boxes that seem to have descended from outer space. Visitors to the cubes are immersed in a nocturnal experience of light and sound. This is the world of Burn, an energy drink developed by Coca-Cola, which is promoting the product in an extraordinary way. The concept for Burn Black Box and 24/7 Night is the work of Dutch design agency Storeage, which numbers Coca-Cola Netherlands, Spain and UK among it's clients.
Burn claims the title of 'world's most potent energy drink'. Coca-Cola wanted a promotional campaign that would launch the brand as the 'must-have energy drink' for clubbers and other 'easygoers'. Whereas Red Bull stresses its association with (extreme) sport, Burn is looking to boost its reputation and market share as a nightlife drink. Inside the inscrutable Black Box, Burn interacts with clients and consumers. The cubes are as cryptic, surprising, exciting and intensely stimulating as the nightlife energized by Burn.
Burn Black Box is a dismountable, 5-cubic-m structure made from steel panels clad in matte-black vinyl on the outside and black mirrors and LEDs on the inside. 'We went for a black cube because of the mysterious, iconic, nocturnal image,' explains Martijn Hoogendijk, creative director of Storeage. 'Underlining the mysterious aspect is the monolithic quality of the black cube, an object invariably seen as a sort of fremdkörper. This powerful geometric form also works in applications like packaging, advertising campaigns and giveaways.'
Inside, it's midnight 24 hours a day. A rousing beat fills the interior. Sensors respond to your presence with a pattern of flickering LEDs on the wall. Moving your body to the music increases the intensity and resolution of lighting and visuals. The climax is the sight of your silhouette bursting into flame. You are in total control.

Sensors react to human movement with a pattern of flickering LEDs on the wall.

Stop moving and everything slows to a grinding halt. The Black Box experience is always different, always exciting. When two or more visitors enter the cube, their combined energy generates a 'flaming' experience of another sort. The average time spent inside is ten minutes.

Product samples were passed out in and outside the box, but remarkably enough, the drink itself does not appear in the campaign. 'It's not about the product and the packaging, but about positioning the brand,' says Hoogendijk. 'We won the pitch because we created a platform for brand and customer to interact.' He compares it to a store where merchandise is replaced by the values, attitude and personality radiated by a certain brand.

Why was retail specialist Storeage asked to do a job that seems more appropriate for an outfit with a focus on communication or event-planning? Hoogendijk shares his thoughts on the distinction between the disciplines: 'Event-planning equals retail. Retail is any platform where interaction between customer and brand takes place. Then, too, Burn Black Box and the 24/7 Night concept transcend the "event" to offer an "experience": the experience that customers have with a brand that wants to sell them its products. And that's our definition of retail. It's more than a shop around the corner or a POS display. Retail equals mind space equals selling space equals retail.'

The Burn Black Box appears in conspicuous outdoor locations: beach, plaza, roundabout. A total of five 'experience boxes' moves into the city in question for a period of one week before being dismantled and moved to the following city. One or two weeks before the cubes arrive at their destination, empty 1-cubic-m boxes are set up across the city – accompanied by a flurry of posters and flyers – to generate speculation and arouse curiosity.

A week before the event begins, a Launch/VIP party – complete with celebrities, hot DJs and other performers – is held in the city in question to announce the happening and to spark media interest. Locations scouted in advance vary from factories and parking garages to seaside and rooftop venues. Available for sales purposes is a VIP Box, slightly smaller than the Black Boxes, which features a lounge area, seating, two small coffee tables and two refrigerators filled with samples of Burn. Staffing this box, which is housed in an indoor location near the party, are sales managers and hostesses whose job is to get key accounts, buzzmakers and potential customers excited about Burn.

The initial launch of Burn Black Box took place in March 2006 at the Westergasfabriek in Amsterdam in the presence of all the European brand managers for Burn and the guests of Coca-Cola Netherlands. The evening opened with the presentation of the concept and the introduction of the Black Box prototype. While enjoying tapas served by sexy models, guests sipped new cocktails based on Burn. A live DJ kept the party going deep into the night, accentuating the payoff line of the Burn campaign: 'Energy and confidence to experience the night to the maximum'.

'We won the pitch because we created a platform for brand and customer to interact.' Martijn Hoogendijk

Designer: Storeage – www.store-age.nl
Photographers: UVA (United Visual Artists), Maarten de Ru – www.deru.nu

Client: Burn – www.coca-cola.com
Consultant: UVA
Manufacturer: Brandwacht en Meijer and Barco
Total floor area (m^2): 25
Duration of construction: 2 days per Black Box
Start of event: 7 March 2006

This page: Moving faster and faster to the music makes the light in the Burn Black Box brighter and the visuals sharper.

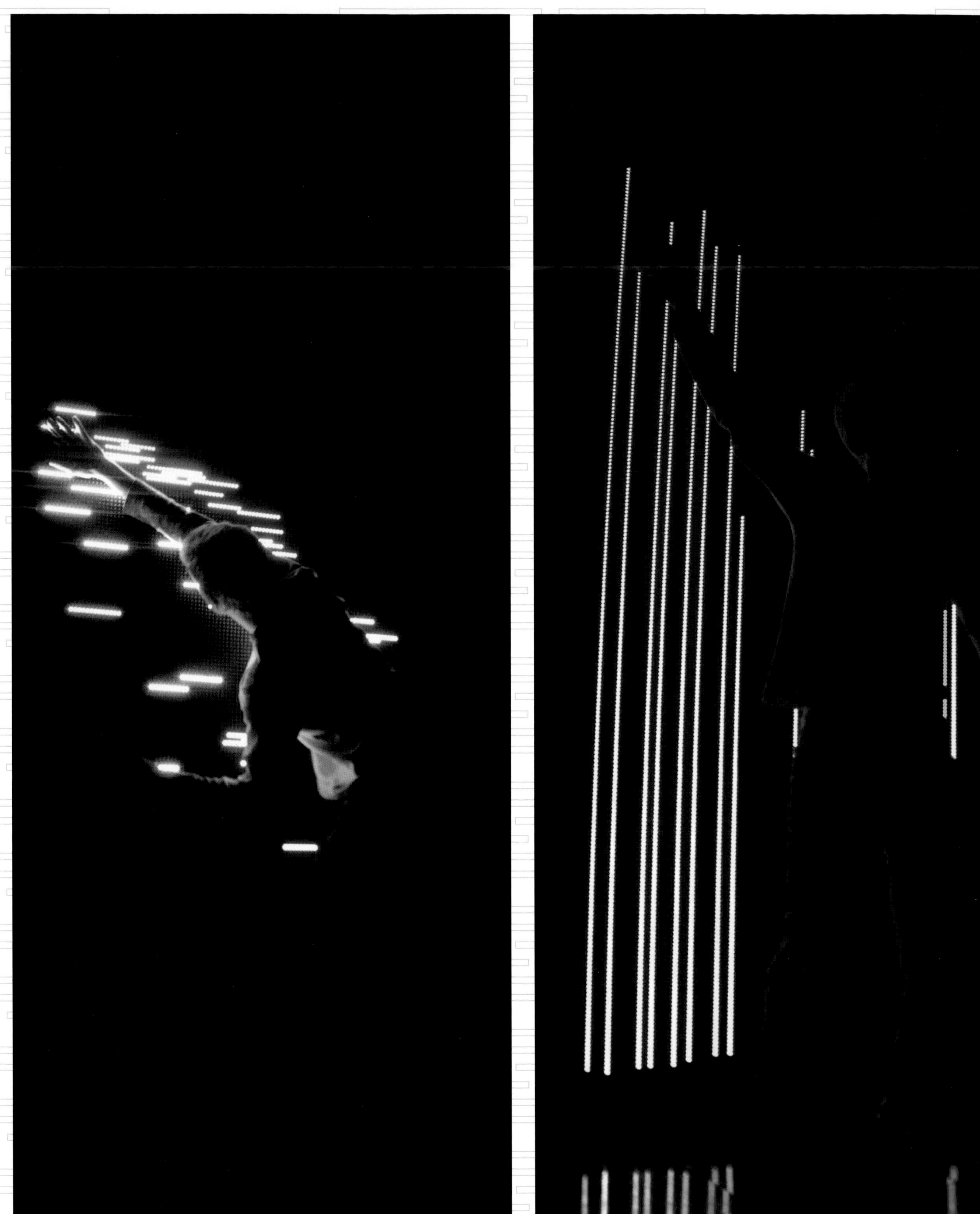

This page: A black, vinyl-covered, VIP box – which houses a lounge with seating, tables and a fridge filled with samples of Burn – can usually be found at an indoor location close to the Launch/VIP party.

This page and opposite: Highlight of the interactive experience is a'fire-fountain explosion' of the participant's silhouette.

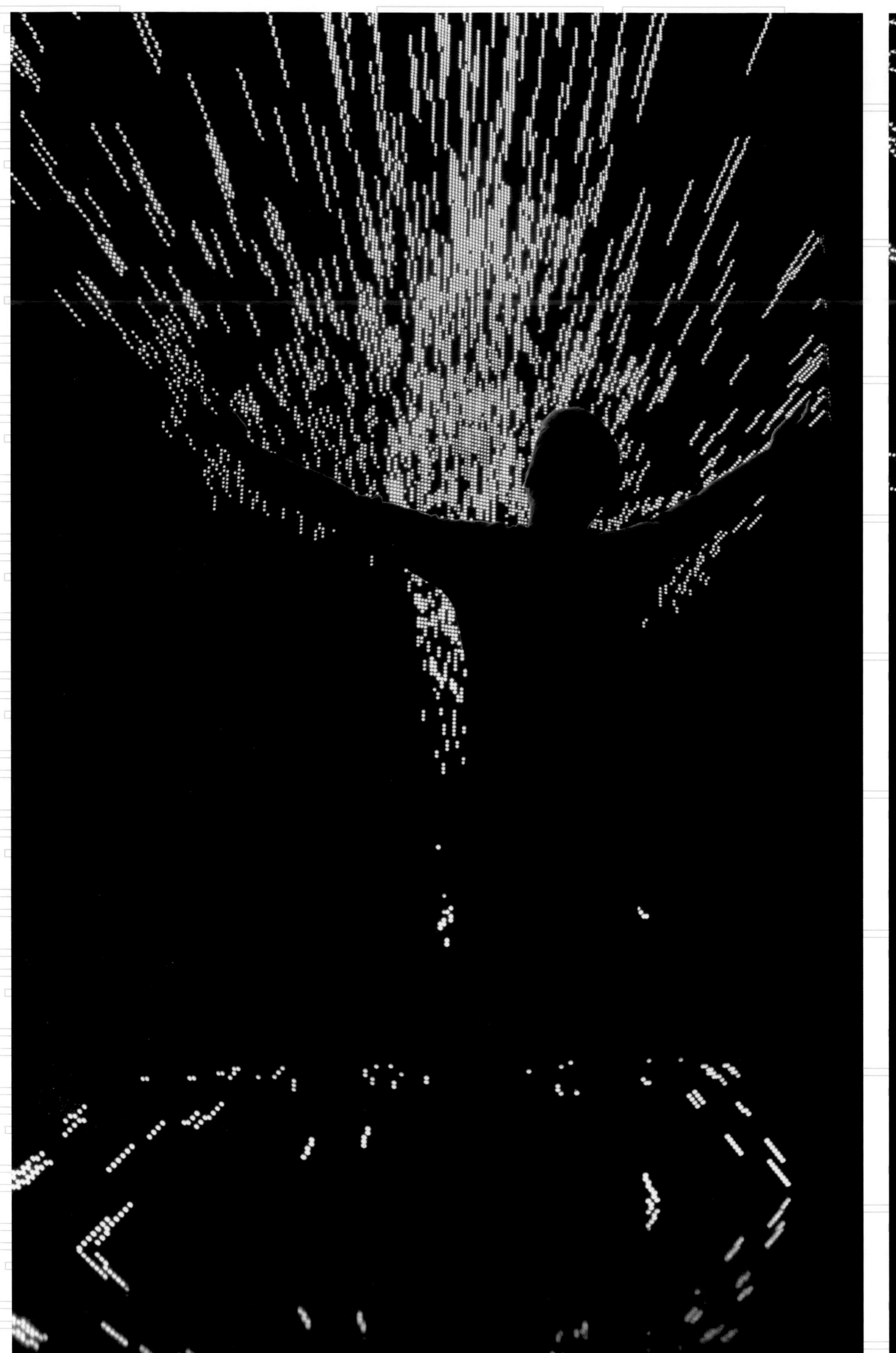

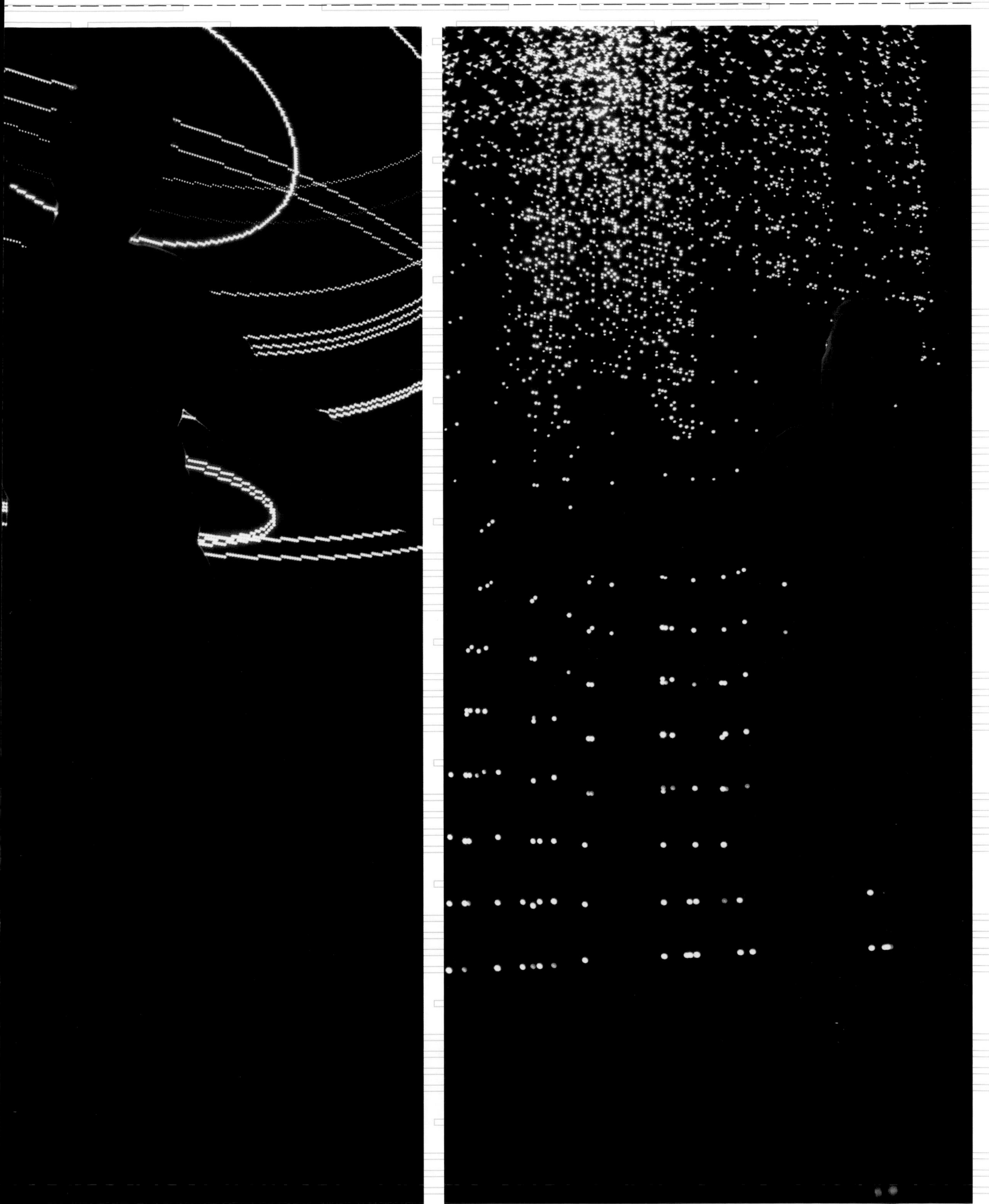

The high point of the two-day event was the re-creation of Nelson's most famous naval battle, made even more exciting by a masterly example of pyrotechnics that could be seen by spectators a full five miles from the coast.

MICE GROUP
TRAFALGAR 200
PORTSMOUTH, UNITED KINGDOM

Rule, Brittania!

Like many large island nations, Great Britain is a land of crusaders, explorers and admirals. Throughout the turbulent, war-torn history of the island, the sea has been its powerful, nearly mythical ally. And this fascination with the sea was still very much in evidence when more then a million spectators gathered on a sultry day in June 2005 to experience the re-enactment of one of naval history's most notable battles. From the shore they watched an impressive sight as hundreds of ships from 36 nations gathered in the Solent bay near Portsmouth. The event was more than just an ambitious opportunity for landlubbers drawn to the sea, and more than a maritime Glastonbury music festival starring an awesome armada. In 2005 Britons celebrated the bicentenary of their victory over the French and Spanish fleets. Not far from Cape Trafalgar, Spain, Admiral Nelson faced Napoleon and proved to be a shrewder strategist than his rival. And, like the battle of Waterloo, this legendary naval skirmish is worthy of a public commemoration. For this reason, Britain's Royal Navy initiated a spectacular event and invited MICE Group to transform its objectives into an impressive two-day experience.
An obvious choice, MICE specializes in creating experiential marketing solutions for the world's leading brands. The venue and scale of a brand experience event may differ substantially from those of more conventional marketing campaigns, but the goal is ultimately the same: communicating a vision and creating a unique and memorable impression. The multifaceted theme chosen by the Royal Navy – Past Glories, Future Horizons – did present MICE with a challenge, however, because the event had to be more than the celebration of a historic naval victory. It was to be a global tribute to the courage of all seamen in the past and present, and a plea for the important role of navies in the future.

A dramatic display by the British RAF's 'Red Arrows' during the International Fleet Review.

The live event would be attended by a crowd of some 1.3 million spectators (including those in surrounding non-core site areas) and broadcast in 150 countries. The large and varied international audience and the extensive objectives put forth by the Royal Navy to embrace all of the different nations and cultures involved in the event demanded a sophisticated programme that would balance spectacle, creativity tradition and ceremony. Although the summer events were pushed off with a formal review of the 167-vessel international fleet by the British Royal Family, the evening programme, brought to life as a son et lumière, was the highlight of the two-day celebration. The unique sound-and-light show was part of a magnificent historical scene – a period re-enactment of the battle of Trafalgar – performed just off the coast of Portsmouth. MICE used an international fleet of 17 tall ships, exact replicas of the vessels that Napoleon and Nelson had commanded during the momentous encounter. A choreographed drama on board the ships began with a cast of 120, featuring actors and real sailors. Stage lights illuminated the decks of the vessels, and searchlights followed the action from the beach. Large screens, a specially-devised three-hour radio play broadcast on BBC Radio Solent, and a dramatic soundtrack that washed up on shore through a series of PA amplifier systems bridged the gap between stage and audience and immersed spectators in an authentic battle experience. The spectacle of roaring cannons, volleys and clouds of gunpowder steered the show towards the finale: a state-of-the-art pyrotechnic display, visible five miles off the coast. 12 tonnes of fireworks and special effects mounted on the tall ships created a truly synchronised, choreographed scene using the latest digital computer technology, silhouetting the battle ships against a vivid backdrop of light and smoke. Concluding the two-day programme was a prestigious International Drumhead Ceremony, held before a seated audience of 10,000 veterans and a party of international VIPs. The ceremony, based on the traditional military service parade of soldiers and drummers, commemorated the sacrifices and casualties of war and promoted international understanding, friendship and reconciliation. Here, MICE united tradition, ceremony, innovation and high-tech to create a service of remembrance to commemorate and reflect on the duty and sacrifice of thousands of maritime men and women in conflicts over the years. The Veterans Centre on the festival grounds allowed old comrades to reunite in peaceful surroundings. Computer facilities were installed to make it easy for the veterans to find one another.

Trafalgar 200 was the largest live public event held in the UK in 2005. It took a great deal of innovation and logistic expertise to physically realize the objectives of the Royal Navy and to produce an extravaganza complete with facilities for a huge number of visitors. The organization of Trafalgar 200 has undoubtedly raised the standard for international public events, and the various creative and logistical aspects of this particular production have been acknowledged by the events industry. The major awards that MICE has won since June 2005 include a Gold ITMA (Incentive Travel & Meetings Association) award, a Victor Ludorum prize, and top honours as the Best Public Event at the Corporate Event Association Awards.

The unique sound-and-light show was part of a magnificent historical scene – a period re-enactment of the battle of Trafalgar – performed on a two-mile-wide floating stage.

Designer: MICE Group – www.micegroup.com
Photography: James Boardman – james@boardmanpix.co.uk

Client: Royal Navy – higham@hambledon2000.freeserve.co.uk
Lighting consultant: MICE International
Graphics consultant: MICE International
Engineer: MICE STD
Manufacturer: MICE Silver Knight
Pyrotechnics: Kimbolton Fireworks
Capacity: 350,000 guests
Duration of construction: 4 weeks
Start of event: 28 June 2005

Veterans and war heroes were honoured in a ceremonial complement to the battle at sea. A grand reunion of old comrades took place in tents which formed a temporary Veterans Centre on the festival grounds.

This page and opposite: With over a million visitors and a programme filled with spectacle and activities, at times Trafalgar 200 evoked images of the sounds and crowds that mark the annual Glastonbury music festival.

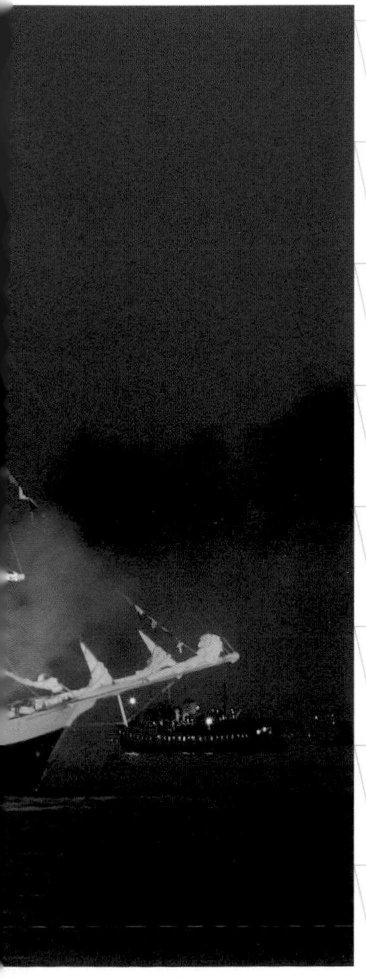

HAPPENING DESIGN FOR EVENTS

Publishers: Frame Publishers – www.framemag.com,
Birkhäuser, Publishers for Architecture – www.birkhauser.ch

Compiled by Tessa Blokland
Editors: Sarah Schultz and Marlous Willems

Introduction by Jeroen Junte

Texts by Anneke Bokern, Joeri Bruyninckx, Andrea Eschbach, Tim Groen, Cornelius Mangold, Edwin van Onna, Stephan Ott, Sarah Martín Pearson, Chris Scott and Masaaki Takahashi

Graphic design: The Stone Twins – www.stonetwins.com

Copy editing: Donna de Vries-Hermansader

Translation: InOtherWords (D'Laine Camp, Donna de Vries-Hermansader), Ella Wildridge

Colour reproduction: Neroc, Amsterdam

Printing: D2Print, Singapore

Distribution:
ISBN 10: 90-77174-22-2
ISBN 13: 978-90-77174-22-7
Frame Publishers, Lijnbaansgracht 87, 1015 GZ Amsterdam, Netherlands
www.framemag.com

ISBN-10: 3-7643-7976-6
ISBN-13: 978-3-7643-7976-6
Birkhäuser – Publishers for Architecture, PO Box 133. 4010 Basel, Switzerland
Part of Springer Science+Business Media
www.birkhauser.ch

A CIP catalogue record for this book is available from the Library of Congress, Washington D.C., USA

Bibliographic information published by Die Deutsche Bibliothek
Die Deutsche Bibliothek lists this publication in the Deutsche Nationalbibliografie; detailed bibliographic data is available in the internet at http://dnb.ddb.de.

Printed on acid-free paper produced from chlorine-free pulp. TCF ∞
Printed in Singapore
987654321